Haunted Montana

A GHOSTHUNTER'S GUIDE TO HAUNTED PLACES YOU CAN VISIT

Karen Stevens

RIVERBEND
PUBLISHING

Haunted Montana
Copyright © 2007 by Karen Stevens

Published by Riverbend Publishing, Helena, Montana

ISBN 10: 1-931832-87-0
ISBN 13: 978-1-931832-87-8

Printed in the United States of America.

1 2 3 4 5 6 7 8 9 0 MG 14 13 12 11 10 09 08 07

Cover design by DD Dowden
Text design by Suzan Glosser

Cataloging-in-Publication data is on file at the Library of Congress.

Riverbend Publishing
P.O. Box 5833
Helena, MT 59604
1-866-787-2363
www.riverbendpublishing.com

Cover image: The very haunted Western Heritage Center in Billings, Montana.

TABLE OF CONTENTS

IN MEMORY OF

JACK TRAVIS

FRIEND, MENTOR, AND GHOST HUNTER EXTRAORDINAIRE

INTRODUCTION

Nearly everyone enjoys tales of ghostly figures and phantom footsteps, especially when told in the reassuring glow of a campfire. But what if phantom footsteps are coming up your basement stairs—and you're home by yourself?

I grew up in a haunted house, and over the years everyone in my family heard those ghostly footsteps climbing our stairs. Eventually we learned to coexist, though somewhat uneasily, with the unseen presence that lurked in the basement and sometimes rattled doorknobs or turned on lights. Because of those experiences I have no doubt that paranormal phenomena do occur. The real questions, in my opinion, are not *if,* but *how* and *why* they occur.

Some say that ghosts are figments of the imagination, or that the phenomena attributed to ghosts are due to faulty observation. Others say that ghosts are a form of emotional energy given off in times of crisis and somehow absorbed by the surroundings. There is growing evidence that low-frequency sound waves that affect a certain section of the brain can produce some of the phenomena. And, of course, ghosts may be just what they've been assumed to be all along: spirits of those who have died. The ghostly voices captured on audiotapes seem to point toward that conclusion, at least in some cases.

Probably no single theory can adequately explain all the different kinds of paranormal phenomena, just as no one theory can explain why some people seem to be aware of ghosts while others are completely oblivious to them. Recent experiments have shown that people who report paranormal experiences are also unusually sensitive to electromagnetic fields, so the ability to sense ghosts may be biological, and, like any of the senses, vary considerably from person to person.

I'm fascinated by ghosts, whatever they may be. For many years I've toured haunted theaters, restaurants, and hotels all over the United States with friends who share my interests. And we're not unique—so many people enjoy visiting haunted sites that offbeat tours have sprung up to meet the demand. In Montana, "spirited" Halloween tours are offered in Bannack, Billings, Butte, Helena, and Virginia City. Don't worry if you can't get to those towns—ghosts can be found just about anywhere in this sprawling state.

Montana's earliest written ghost stories date from the era of the fur trappers and roaming bands of Native Americans. In the 1880s the *Billings Gazette* reported that the Crow Indians claimed to have seen the ghosts of a party of white men—presumably those of the Lewis and Clark Expedition—camped at Pompey's Pillar, where William Clark had carved his signature into the rock in 1806. In the 1890s a train engineer reported seeing the ghost of a bleeding man along the railroad tracks between Reed Point and Greycliff. The ghost may have been one of the Thomas wagon train party, killed by Indians in 1866.

Traces of Montana's miners are found, and not only near the tailings left near abandoned mines. The young men who saw the ghost of a miner in worn nineteenth-century clothing along the trail to the ghost town of Independence, high in the Gallatin National Forest, will never forget it. On cold winter nights honkytonk music sometimes can be heard from one of the deserted saloons in the former mining town of Garnet.

The Roaring Twenties gave birth to another crop of ghost stories, among them the tale of three mysterious strangers who became known as the Guardians of the Hi-Line. One bitterly cold winter day in the late 1920s a resident of Browning was driving on a deserted country road when his car slid into a snowdrift. Unable to move the car by himself, the driver was rescued by three strangers who quickly pushed the stalled car out of the snowdrift. Both vehicles then headed for Browning. When the rescued man reached the safety of town, he turned in the driver's seat to wave thanks to his rescuers. They had vanished, leaving no tracks in the snow.

Ghostly encounters continued to be reported throughout the following decades. In the 1950s, unexplained phenomena began to be documented at the Little Bighorn National Battlefield where Lt. Col. George Armstrong Custer and over 200 men of the 7th Cavalry died in 1876. And in the 1970s, two long-haul truck drivers saw *and heard* a phantom wagon train creaking across the prairie not far from present-day Hysham.

In the 1990s, a phantom warrior on horseback reportedly galloped after two BLM employees and their dog as they drove away from Pompey's Pillar at the end of a day's work. At a certain point on the road, the ghost vanished, leaving the men stunned and the dog cowering. More recently, a man who often drives Highway 200 from Jordan to Lewistown saw a phantom motorcyclist on a Harley surrounded by a glowing light. Although the driver of the car tried to catch up, the phantom effortlessly kept ahead of the pursuing car. A few weeks later, the same driver *and his passenger* saw the ghostly motorcyclist along the same stretch of road. And the owners of a home near Canyon Creek Battlefield were plagued one winter by demanding knocks at their door, only to find no one there and no tracks in the fresh snow. Perhaps the unseen visitor is the ghostly soldier in 1870s military uniform who appeared once in their hallway.

Why should the Treasure State have such a treasure trove of ghosts? Life on the frontier was rough and frequently dangerous, all too often cut short by accidents or violence. Men lived hard, played hard and—sometimes—died hard. If energy truly cannot be destroyed, it is little wonder that restless spirits from those turbulent days linger even now on the battlefields and in the dimly lit corridors of historic buildings and private homes across the state. Are those hotels, saloons, railroad depots, and museums *really* haunted? People who work or live in them claim to have had some pretty strange experiences over the years, and I have no reason to doubt them.

Nearly all of those people take their ghosts matter-of-factly, or even with a touch of quiet pride, like at Chico Hot Springs Resort where the ghost of former owner Percie Knowles has appeared in the crowded dining room. And why shouldn't they? Montana's ghosts are, after all, part of Montana's history.

My files contain hundreds of ghost stories collected over 25 years. I've chosen those that offer the best of both worlds for this book: publicly accessible sites of historic interest plus current ghostly activity. Since part of the fun of visiting haunted sites is the possibility of encountering a ghost, I've also rated each site according to the level of paranormal activity experienced by those who work or live there. A "low" rating indicates that activity is sporadic and infrequent, "moderate" means activity occurs occasionally, and "high" indicates that visitors have often reported ghostly experiences.

I've included stories from all over the state, from eerie Belton Chalet in West Glacier to the poignant tale of the haunted Little Cowboy Bar in Fromberg. Most of the stories have never before been made public. Along the way I've met hundreds of wonderful people who graciously shared their stories with me. Many thanks to them, and also to my "ghost researchers" Dan Damjanovich and Cynthia Berst of Billings, and Mary Doerk of Fort Benton, who have enthusiastically tracked down ghost stories for me. Special thanks to the unseen person at the Montana Territorial Prison—perhaps "Turkey Pete" Eitler himself, long-dead resident of the prison—whose voice on tape gently corrected my mispronunciation of his name... from the Other Side!

Please join me now as we go in search of the ghosts of the Treasure State!

HAUNTED
ANACONDA

COPPER VILLAGE MUSEUM
401 East Commercial
Anaconda, Montana 59711
Telephone: 406-563-2422

Ghostly Activity Level: High

HISTORY: The Anaconda City Hall was built in 1896 to house the fire department, the police station, and city government. The building was abandoned in 1976 but saved from demolition by the timely intervention of local residents who cherished its eclectic mixture of classical, Roman, Moorish, and Gothic architecture. Today, the old city hall is home to the Copper Village Museum and Art Center.

PHENOMENA: The building has a long history of haunting, dating back to 1901 when police officers in the basement jail office repeatedly heard footsteps in the empty corridors above them. No one ever was found, despite lengthy investigation. The ghost is thought to be a prisoner who had died in his cell in February 1901. Firemen stationed in the building also heard the footsteps. Present-day staff at the Copper Village Museum report doors that mysteriously lock or unlock, a strong sense of presence, footsteps, and items being moved from one place to another.

I arrived at the old city hall in Anaconda with my friends Frank and Sue early on a Saturday morning to find dozens of people busily setting up booths for a harvest festival. Carol Jette, director of the museum, was simultaneously directing volunteers and fielding phone calls, but she cheerfully sat down with me for a few minutes to share some of the eerie experiences she'd had in the building.

Jette has been associated with the museum for 21 years. She was aware of the ghost from the very beginning. "When we moved down from the courthouse and started to refurbish this building," she began, "I felt there was a presence right away. When we were in here working, mysterious things would happen. There were footsteps when no one was in the building, doors would shut by themselves, and sometimes things were moved and brought back days later.

"At first we had our offices down where the gallery is now. About two years ago we moved our office to our present space, and the ghost was not happy. He started doing some numbers on me. I'd use my key in the front door and it wouldn't work. Then I'd come around to the back door and it would work. I'd come through the building to the front door and the key would work. This went on for about two weeks. Finally one day I got angry and confronted him. I said aloud, 'I don't know what you're doing but it's not fun anymore.'

"And it stopped. My key worked from then on. Gradually the feeling got better, as if he had accepted us up there. But people have really felt him upstairs and in the basement."

Others who previously knew nothing about the ghost have encountered it, as well.

"We had a plumber come in one day," Jette said, "and he was working in the boiler room. He came upstairs just white as a sheet and asked if there was someone else in the building. My co-director and I knew he must have encountered the ghost, so we told him the story. He said, 'As long as I know that, I'm okay, I can deal with it.' He had felt a very strong presence down there. Some people have seen shadows where there shouldn't have been shadows. I've never seen them, but I'd love to."

Who is the ghost? Jette doesn't believe it is the prisoner who died in a police cell in 1901. "I've always been under the impression that it was someone who worked here," she stated. "Someone who had strong ties to the building. He is very much trying to protect this building. It's like he's inspecting what we do and then he's happy with the results. I've been told a fireman was injured here and passed away. I've felt him everywhere in the building. Several months ago there were doors closing again upstairs. I walked up there, thinking maybe some kids had gotten in, although I try to keep the stairway door locked. There wasn't anyone there. That's happened many times."

Jette offered to take us to the second floor, and we quickly accepted. I felt my hair stand on end as we entered what had been an imposing courtroom (now used mostly for storage), although nothing unusual was visible. Beyond the courtroom was what had been the firemen's dormitory, complete with brackets for the vanished pole. The fire chief's apartment was off to one side.

"There have been people who walked into the fire chief's apartment and backed out, saying they couldn't go in," Jette remarked. "I think it's fascinating, and it doesn't scare me one bit. If I ever see him, I think it would frighten me for a moment. I've even talked to him and told him I wouldn't mind seeing him. He just does strange things to us, comical things, nothing ever serious. He loves playing jokes on people."

Downstairs, the harvest festival was about to open to the public, and Jette was urgently needed. Before heading back down the stairs, she gave us permission to take as much time as we needed to look around. Frank, Sue, and I wandered from room to room, snapping photos at random. I was standing in the middle of the courtroom when I suddenly felt my entire left side turn icy. I asked Frank to take a quick digital photo. It showed an orb to my left, almost touching me. Had the orb, considered by many to be a form of ghostly energy, caused that sudden sense of chill? There certainly were no drafts detectable from the huge arched windows.

I decided to speak aloud to any spirits present, hoping to capture a ghostly voice on audiotape. Sure enough, when I replayed the tape, I could make out unintelligible whispers as well as a word that sounded like "Tippit" or "Tibbet."

According to an article entitled "Ghostly Stories Haunt Anaconda's Old City Hall" in the *Montana Standard* of October 31, 2002, several men had lost their lives in the building over the course of the years. No one named "Tibbet" was listed among them. Perhaps a search of old city directories would reveal whether anyone by that name had ever been employed there as a policeman, a fireman, or a member of the judiciary.

Whoever he was, the ghostly prankster of the Copper Village Museum continues to make his presence known from time to time. Why not stop by to enjoy the exhibits? If you feel an icy breeze move past on a warm summer's day, don't worry—it's just the ghost.

The Copper Village Museum is not the only site of a haunting in Anaconda. The Anaconda Copper Company smelter also was haunted. In the late 1970s the ghost of a man dressed in old-fashioned workman's clothing was seen in the concentrator building.

James Hooper began his career at the smelter in 1968 and worked there for decades. He saw the ghost after he had been transferred to the Local Tram Department. "I was working alone up in the old Anaconda Concentrator building, more commonly called 'the mill,'" he told me. "The unit was closed for production but various flux material for the roasting process was stored in silo-type bins in the mill. My job was to 'cork' railroad hopper cars with old rags for loading silica rock and lime rock. I had my lunch with me and during my lunch break I took a short nap on an old bench on the rod mill floor. I suddenly awoke to see an older gentleman in bib overalls walk by. I thought nothing of it until I realized he was wearing an old cloth cap of the type everyone wore on the smelter long ago, instead of the hard hat we were required to wear on the job indoors or out.

"While I have heard of ghost sightings from some of the old miners working underground in the Butte operations, I never thought I'd spot one at the smelter. To my thinking he is probably continuing to work at his assigned task, having worked up on the "Hill" since high school. Many individuals did the same, with their only break in service in forty-five or so years being for military service."

Not long after Hooper contacted me about his sighting, I happened to run across an article that may explain the ghost he saw. According to "Shot in Back by Inventor" published in the *Billings Gazette* on July 22, 1902, a man named John McGeary shot and killed his supervisor, William J. Evans Sr., at the smelter. McGeary, who had invented an improved rack, wanted Evans to try it at the smelter. Evans had refused, saying that he was satisfied with the old method. McGeary also blamed Evans for an injury McGeary had suffered at the concentrators in June. After the shooting, Evans' family was hastily called to the hospital, but he died that night.

I asked Hooper whether the ghost he saw might have been from the early 1900s, and he replied, "This could possibly explain my sighting. I do believe the clothing I saw would fit the early twentieth century. Work clothes didn't change much. The old white duck-cloth caps were referred to in town as a smelterman's cap. This was like a golfer wore. It could very well have been the old supervisor I saw, as he was not carrying tools of any kind."

The Anaconda Copper Company began operations in 1884 and closed in 1980. The buildings have since been demolished and the Old Works Golf Course now occupies the site. The stack still stands in Smelter Park, and at 585 feet can be seen from miles away. Does the spirit of William Evans still linger in the area, brooding on his murder, or has he finally punched out on the time clock of life and gone onward? Perhaps we'll find out someday.

THE LITTLE GIRL AT THE MEADE HOTEL

BANNACK STATE PARK
Bannack, Montana
406-834-3413

Ghostly Activity Level: Moderate

HISTORY: Bannack, the first territorial capital of Montana, was founded in 1862 when gold was discovered in Grasshopper Creek. A gold rush followed, and in its glory days more than 10,000 miners worked streams in the area. Although Virginia City took over as territorial capital in 1865, Bannack continued to exist as a mining town until the 1930s. By the 1950s the town was abandoned. It now is managed as a state park by the Montana Department of Fish, Wildlife & Parks. Over 60 original buildings still stand, and most can be explored.

Bannack probably is best known for its one-time sheriff, Henry Plummer, alleged leader of a gang of vicious robbers. In December 1863, determined to end the reign of terror, a group of men banded together to become the Montana Vigilantes. Within months, the robber gang had been broken up and over 20 of them hanged, including the sheriff.

PHENOMENA: The ghost of a young girl named Dorothy Dunn, who drowned in nearby Grasshopper Creek in 1916, haunts the Meade Hotel. Visitors have seen and heard the ghosts of several children who died of illness at the Bessette House. Visitors have captured ghostly voices on audiotape. Inexplicable cold spots are sometimes felt, even on hot summer days.

Park Ranger John Phillips doesn't believe in ghosts. He has worked for the Montana Department of Fish, Wildlife & Parks for eight years, and has spent several nights alone at Bannack State Park. Although he has heard odd noises, he attributes them to the wind. His skepticism doesn't keep him from collecting ghost stories, however, and Bannack's visitors don't hesitate to share their experiences with him.

"I talked to a man and his little boy who said they were here a couple of years ago," Phillips told me as we stood just inside the entrance of the Meade Hotel. "They had walked into town. There were no tracks in the snow, no cars, and they said they felt they were the only ones here. They went into the school, and when they came out, the merry-go-round was going around in circles, and there were still no tracks.

"They walked across the street to the hotel, and the boy and his dad got separated. The boy went into one of the rooms and 'Dorothy' was standing there laughing at him, like she was the one playing jokes on him and spinning the merry-go-round."

Phillips continued, "Another day I was panning gold in our tubs next to the Bessette House. There was a large group of people watching the demonstration, and two of the chaperones decided they didn't really care about gold-panning, so they went into the Bessette House. They came out very quickly and they were really upset. They said they saw children sitting in the stairwell.

"The Bessette House is called the Crying Baby House. The story is that nine children died there during an epidemic, and some people claim they've heard the babies crying.

"Another time, a lady said she used to come here in the 1960s. She and her friends brought a Ouija board, and an image of a man appeared. They thought it was Henry Plummer."

Plummer might have good reason to haunt the place, given his violent death at the hands of the Vigilantes and the doubt that still exists over his guilt, but most of the paranormal activity seems to focus on the Meade Hotel. The hotel was built in 1875 as a courthouse, then it served as a hotel from 1890 to the 1930s. The imposing building has an elegantly curved staircase that leads to the upper floors. I decided to explore it. Halfway up the stairs, I felt something icy-cold pass behind me, chilling my back. The day was hot, and the hotel pleasantly warm inside. I could find no rational explanation for the chill I had felt. Had "Dorothy" just made her presence known?

I continued up the staircase to the second floor. My friend Sue Tracy was already there, hoping to capture something abnormal on film.

The second floor proved a disappointment. If "Dorothy" was there, she seemed to be avoiding us. We started back toward the stairs again, only to find another party coming up with their golden retriever in tow. We decided to follow them, to see whether the dog reacted to anything we couldn't see. Again we were disappointed; the dog's actions seemed perfectly normal. Sue and I then decided to explore the schoolhouse across the street. I took a good look at the merry-go-round that apparently spun by itself at times. There was a strong breeze blowing that afternoon, but the merry-go-round was stationary. I gave it a tentative shove, which barely caused it to move a few inches. It would obviously take considerable effort to make the rusted machine turn. Perhaps a strong gale was blowing the day the boy and his father had seen it move by itself—or perhaps the ghost of "Dorothy" had indeed caused it to turn.

We strolled down the dusty street toward the Bessette House. The building apparently had been used as a dwelling longer than most of the buildings at Bannack, because linoleum still covered the floor of one of the rooms. I cautiously climbed the narrow, creaking stairway where two of John Phillip's tour group had seen a group of ghostly children sitting, and took a few photos of the large, empty room upstairs. My digital camera captured a couple of orbs—the balls of light energy that often are found in haunted places—but that was all. The fretful, crying babies didn't make a peep while we were there.

Tired and somewhat disappointed, we walked back to the visitor center, where we overheard an excited woman telling a friend about the ghost she had just seen—an older man wearing an antique Stetson hat. He had a long white beard and was leaning against one of the buildings. She had taken her eyes off him just for a moment, and he had vanished.

Just then, my friend Frank walked in. He has a long white beard and wears an old Stetson. The woman saw him and turned white. "That's the ghost!" she exclaimed.

Frank, never at a loss, made her a courtly bow. He explained that he had gotten tired of walking around in the heat and decided to sit in the shade to wait for Sue and me. When he saw us approaching, he had simply gotten up and started toward the visitor center, where we had agreed to meet. At that, all of us, including the woman who had mistaken him for a ghost, burst out laughing. At least that was one ghost story we could disprove on the spot!

Many ghost stories are so vague—a cold chill, a sense of presence—that it's impossible to track down a historical basis for a haunting. The case of the young girl who drowned in Grasshopper Creek seemed a bit more substantial, however, so I decided to see whether I could find an account of the tragedy. John Phillips had mentioned that the drowning had occurred in 1916, and sure enough, I found an August 16, 1916, article entitled "Young Girl is Drowned" in the *Dillon Examiner*, reporting an incident that had occurred on August 7: "A most deplorable accident occurred at two o'clock last Friday afternoon when Dorothy Dunn, a sixteen year old girl, met her death by drowning, and had it not been for the bravery and forethought of Smith Paddock, a twelve-year-old boy, Ruth Wornick and Fern Dunn, a sister of the unfortunate girl, would have met the same fate.

"The three girls had gone to Grasshopper creek just on the outskirts of Bannack to wade and bathe in the creek. They waded out into a hole dug out by one of the old dredging boats, not realizing their danger. Suddenly all three stepped off of a ledge into nine feet of water. None of the girls were able to swim. Smith Paddock was passing along the road and seeing the girls floundering in the water ran to their assistance, getting there just as Dorothy went down, never to come to the surface alive again. Young Paddock could swim but could not dive and was unable to reach Dorothy, so he turned his attention to the other two girls and after a long hard struggle saved them both.

"The body of Dorothy Dunn was recovered several hours afterwards. The funeral was held Saturday at Bannack and was attended by the whole countryside. Interment was made in the burying ground at the old capital. Miss Dunn was the daughter of Mrs. Edward Dunn of Bannack and had lived in that town about a year. During her brief residence in the thriving little mining camp she had made many warm friends and the news of her tragic death came as a shock to them."

The spirit of Dorothy Dunn was seen not long after her death, according to author F. Lee Graves, former resident of Bannack. Graves' godmother, Bertie Matthews, had been Dunn's friend and the two girls had often played in the hotel where Bertie's mother worked. Several years after the drowning, Bertie saw Dorothy's ghost wearing a long blue dress, on the second floor of the Meade Hotel. Since then, many people have seen or sensed her presence.

If you visit Bannack in search of ghosts, don't overlook the old jail. Recently an entire family heard the sound of ghostly sobbing coming from the empty building.

THE SPIRITS OF BIG HOLE
NATIONAL BATTLEFIELD

BIG HOLE NATIONAL BATTLEFIELD
West of Wisdom, Montana
406-689-3155

Ghostly Activity Level: Low

HISTORY: In the pre-dawn darkness of August 9, 1877, U.S. soldiers attacked 800 Nez Perce Indians camped along the Big Hole River. Gold had been discovered near their homelands in Idaho, Oregon, and Washington a few years earlier, and a new treaty drawn up that sharply reduced the size of their reservation. Many of the Nez Perce refused to agree to the treaty and fled the area, pursued by the Army under the command of Colonel John Gibbon. They crossed into Montana in late July and made camp on August 7 among the willows that grew along the Big Hole River. The exhausted Indians thought they were temporarily safe from pursuit and could rest their footsore horses and gather food to replenish their supplies.

The next day the Nez Perce set up tepees on the willow flats. The women cut lodge poles while some of the men went hunting. Others cared for the horses or cleaned weapons. They didn't set guards, for the Nez Perce believed they were in friendly territory. One of the Nez Perce children later recalled that, as dusk fell, many children played a noisy stick game near the creek.

Troops crept up on them during the night, however, intending to attack at dawn. An old Indian man stumbled onto the concealed soldiers when he rose early to check on his horses. He was immediately killed, and those shots roused the village. The Army killed over 90 Indians, many of them women and children who were fleeing into the willow brush in a futile attempt to escape. Also killed were 22 Army soldiers and six civilians.

The Nez Perce warriors finally managed to drive the soldiers out of camp. They had no time to grieve. The next day, after hastily burying the dead, the surviving Nez Perce fled, bereft, with essentially no food or shelter. On a freezing cold September 30 the Army again caught up with them at Bear Paw, where they were camped only 40 miles from refuge across the Canadian border. The Army drove off most of their horses and, after a siege lasting days, Chief Joseph surrendered on October 5 with the memorable words: "Hear me, my chiefs! My heart is sick and sad. From where the sun now stands I will fight no more forever."

PHENOMENA: Descendents of the Nez Perce who were present at the Big Hole battle state that they can sense and sometimes even hear the spirits of those who died there. National Park Service employees report that tourists sometimes break down in tears at the site. A few have claimed to sense the spirits of the dead around them. A visitor who does historical re-enactments heard many voices as he made his way through the willows. A number of eerie things have occurred during significant anniversaries of the battle.

We had just started driving up the spectacular Chief Joseph Pass on our way to the Big Hole Battlefield when I became aware of a growing sense of unease coupled with an almost overwhelming urge to turn around and look back down the trail. At first I attributed it to my dislike of steep passes, with their treacherous switchbacks and sheer drops, but this was far more intense than I had previously experienced. The closer we got to the top of the pass, the worse it grew, until I was almost sick with apprehension. Then, as the road began to descend into the broad valley of the Big Hole River, the apprehension vanished and a great sense of relief took its place.

Was it a normal reaction to the steep road? Probably. I don't claim to enjoy mountain driving. What I didn't know at the time, however, was that in 1877 the fleeing Nez Perce had crossed the mountains just one ridge over. They must have watched their back trail apprehensively, watching with dread for the first signs of pursuit. When their scouts reported that the soldiers apparently had given up, the relief must have been overwhelming.

They left behind an echo of the terrible events that occurred in the predawn darkness of August 9, 1877. Wilfred Otis Halfmoon, a Nez Perce whose great-grandfather was killed during the battle, worked as a cultural interpreter at the battlefield for several years and said that he often could feel the spirits of the dead around him. In *Big Sky Ghosts Vol. 2* by Debra D. Munn (Pruett Publishing Company, 1994), Halfmoon talked about an experience he and a friend had at Big Hole National Battlefield in the 1960s. The two young men were visiting the battlefield with a church group and decided to camp overnight beside the river. At first all was quiet, but after a while they began to hear disturbing noises.

"Later we began to hear women crying, babies squalling, and then a terrible screaming," Halfmoon told Munn. The two boys climbed up the hill where the Nez Perce horses had been pastured before the battle and looked back toward the campground. They could see nothing, but the eerie sounds continued.

"They were noises I never wanted to hear again," Halfmoon said. "Even today I can still feel the presence of those people. I don't hear the sounds as much any more, not like I used to. Most of the Nez Perce don't like talking about such things, but I know that others have had the same experience."

On rare occasions, non-Native American visitors have heard inexplicable noises on the battlefield, though not the sounds of the battle itself. Jeff and his wife Natalie are historical re-enactors who add to the colorful Wild West atmosphere in Virginia City and Nevada City each summer. They enjoy visiting historic sites and over the years have had a number of uncanny experiences.

One of those incidents occurred the day Jeff visited Big Hole Battlefield. He had left the trail and was picking his way through the scattered clumps of willows along the banks of the Big Hole River when he began to hear voices.

"I knew I was the only visitor down there," he told me, "but I could hear the sounds of a village, with children's laughter and people calling to one another. I couldn't make out the words. Then I started to hear a 'huffing' noise in the bushes around me. I've heard white-tailed bucks huff at me during hunting season, but I looked around and nothing was there."

The voices instantly ceased when Jeff stepped out of the willows onto the trail. There was no village, no children playing. When he returned to the visitor center he mentioned his experience to a ranger, who didn't seem surprised. "I got the feeling that the ranger had heard similar accounts from visitors before," Jeff said.

Had Jeff somehow stepped back in time to the day before the attack? Or was this a residual haunting in which the tragic events somehow impressed themselves on the surroundings, to be replayed whenever someone of sensitivity is nearby?

Robert and Carol Lampe of Butte also had an odd experience when they visited the battlefield during the week commemorating the 128th anniversary of the battle. The couple had been dating for a while but had not yet become engaged.

On August 5, 2005, they walked to where the village had been in 1877. Robert said, "While sitting in the center of the village, Carol said that she could hear voices, as if a lot of people were present. At that moment, I felt compelled to 'pop the question.' Carol instantly replied, 'Yes.' No sooner did she reply than a pair of sandhill cranes flew right over us. At the same time, Carol said that she could hear people cheering, and then all became silent. We took the strange occurrence as an omen, and the next day asked a Nez Perce elder about it. He broke into a large smile and said it was a very good omen." The couple subsequently married on Christmas Day, 2005.

Their experience, and the apparent reaction of the voices to Robert's proposal, seems to indicate that there may be more than just a residual haunting at the Big Hole Battlefield.

I decided to ask a ranger about ghosts at the battlefield, even though National Park Service employees are usually reluctant to speak publicly about ghosts at our national parks.

Ranger Tim Fisher listened quietly as I told him about Jeff's experience. "I haven't experienced anything ghostly myself," he said. "I've heard that the Nez Perce can hear sounds, but I've been out there in the middle of the night and didn't hear anything."

He was silent for a moment. "There were a couple of things that occurred that make you think, however. One year we set up a tepee to commemorate the anniversary of the battle. It was the first time in a long while that the native people had put up a lodge down on the battlefield. There were probably 125 people out there doing that, and 300 people up at the visitor center. There was a powwow going on, and children running around. As soon as we put that lodge up down below in the Nez Perce Camp, a little whirlwind came up and lifted the demonstration tepee located near the visitor center off the ground, carried it about five feet, and dropped it. There were five kids under the tepee.

"The Nez Perce tell a story of how five children were killed in a lodge down there. When this tepee was lifted and dropped, it didn't touch anybody. With all these people milling around, no one was harmed. It lifted up high enough to go over the kids' heads that were playing in the tepee."

Fisher continued, "On the hundred-twenty-fifth anniversary we did a candlelight vigil. We put the number of candles for soldiers wounded or killed around the monument, and about ninety in the Nez Perce camp. We did that until about eleven-thirty or so. A couple hundred people came and walked out to the camp. Then we got the radio call to close it all out, and we went and blew out all the candles. Just as we blew out the last candle, this big meteor came, *whoosh!* It just lit up the whole sky like daylight. It lit up the whole trail. The timing was eerie."

He paused, and added, "I guess we did the right thing."

The Big Hole National Battlefield is a site of tragedy and should be approached with respect. The anniversary of the battle is an especially poignant time, when descendents of both the Nez Perce and of the soldiers who died in the battle come together to seek understanding.

FOOTPRINTS IN
THE ATTIC

WESTERN HERITAGE CENTER
2822 Montana Avenue
Billings, Montana 59101
406-256-6809

Ghostly Activity Level: High

HISTORY: The gray turreted building on Montana Avenue was built in 1901 as a memorial to Parmly Billings, son of the railroad magnate Frederick Billings. Parmly had been sent to Montana to look after his father's business interests in Billings. When he unexpectedly died at age 25, his family donated the building that became the young city's first public library. The Parmly Billings Memorial Library served the community well until the 1960s, when it became obvious that the library's needs had outgrown the building. The library moved to larger quarters in 1969 and the old building was abandoned. It sat empty, gradually deteriorating, for several years. If it hadn't been for a group of concerned citizens, the building would have been razed and replaced by a parking lot. It became the Western Heritage Center in 1971, specializing in the history of the Yellowstone River valley.

PHENOMENA: Child-sized footprints were found in the dust

of the attic. The ghostly figure of an elderly woman was seen in 1976 and again in the mid-1990s. In 2003, a staff member and two interns saw the ghost of an elderly man seated in an armchair near the fireplace in the basement. Footsteps cross the floor when only the caretaker is in the building. The theater's sound system mysteriously played music even though it was turned off. During a "ghost tour," a rock dislodged itself from a pile and rolled across the floor.

It was a beautiful Saturday afternoon, sunny and unusually warm for late October, and the Haunted Historic Billings trolley tour was going well. We had stopped at the Western Heritage Center to hear long-time employee Al Gehring tell us about "Priscilla," the ghost of a young girl whose footprints had been found in the dust of the attic floor. When he finished, he invited those who dared to follow him up the steep winding stairs to the tower, where they could peer through a hatch into the attic. The more fainthearted among us milled around on the main floor, looking at exhibits.

Not far from me stood a replica of a tall ranch gate with a cattle grid. Stacked neatly at the base of each of the uprights were dozens of gray river rocks, some as large as grapefruit. As one woman approached the gate, a heavy rock detached from the top of the pile and bumped across the polished wooden floor ahead of her. I heard excited chatter as the others discussed what had just happened.

We inspected the remaining rocks. They seemed to be securely in place. I wondered whether the tramping of our group might have caused vibrations that dislodged the rock. To test my theory, I set the rock back on top of the pile, then several of us jumped up and down to see if we could jolt it loose. It stayed firmly in place. Vibrations were likely not the answer. Perhaps "Priscilla" had decided to attract our attention in a rather dramatic way!

The first hints of a haunting at the Western Heritage Center may have come as early as the 1950s. According to librarian Myrtle Cooper, the building had an unsettling atmosphere at times, and no one liked to go up to the attic to fetch old newspapers stored there. Cooper believed that the noises from the attic were due to the wind, but other staff members weren't so sure.

In 1969 the library moved to larger quarters, and the building stood empty for two years before it became the Western Heritage Center. The staff of the new museum noticed unusual noises in the building, including the meowing of a cat, but it wasn't until 1976 that a ghost actually was seen. Tom Posey, the museum's director, was alone in the building at the time, seated at the front desk. He recounted his experience in the in-house newsletter: "I heard a rustling noise and looked up in time to see an elderly figure in a long dress hurry into the Will James Room. I jumped up in quick pursuit, but found the room empty. I knew then that I had met our noisemaker."

Posey's wife also had a close encounter with the ghost. When she stopped in one day, she distinctly felt an invisible something brush past her. The staff named the ghost "Priscilla," though that name now is used for the ghost of the little girl who began to make her presence known a few years later.

Al Gehring handles maintenance and security for the building, and often works there alone after hours. He realized the building was haunted soon after he began working there in 1980. One day he went up to the attic to work on air conditioning units. He found child-sized footprints on the dusty wooden walkways. "It looked as if someone was tiptoeing around," he said. "They were bare feet."

He has heard doors slam, and footsteps. "One day, about closing time, I realized I hadn't set the alarm. I went back in, saw that one of the office doors was open, and closed it, then went downstairs to check everything again. I heard another door slam hard. I ran back upstairs, but all the doors were closed and no one was there."

On a chilly January evening I met with various members of the staff for a tour of the haunted building. We began in the basement, since it triggered a feeling of unease in staff members Ann Kooistra-Manning and Michelle Caron. While we were in the room that formerly had been the children's room of the old library, we noticed that the temperature was dropping. I set down my tape recorder in order to take a few photos, and when I picked it up again I found that it had stopped running, despite fresh batteries and plenty of tape. Ann's tape recorder also malfunctioned in that room.

We examined the other rooms, coming lastly to the theater. As soon as Ann's husband Kevin unlocked the door we heard the faint sound of music. It sounded like a local radio station. Kevin left to check the theater's sound system, and returned a few minutes later shaking his head. The sound system had been turned off at closing *and was still turned off.* Impossible, yet we all had heard the music.

We trooped back upstairs. I checked my video camera, which I had set up to monitor the main floor while we were in the basement. It had quit running after only a few minutes of tape had been exposed, although there was plenty of tape left. Batteries were not the problem because it was plugged into a socket.

The building had still more phenomena in its repertoire, as I learned a few days later when I returned to talk to Darla Bruner. Darla had worked at the Western Heritage Center for about eighteen months.

"It was about ten o'clock at night," she said. "I heard footsteps out there. I called out, 'Kevin? Al? Is that you?' and nobody answered. Then I started hearing noises back in the two offices that adjoin mine. It sounded like books being taken off a shelf. When I went in there, it stopped. Nobody was there. When I sat back down again, though, it started up again, this time in Kevin's office."

"Priscilla" and the elderly female apparently are not the only ghosts at the Western Heritage Center. In 2002, a young intern who had not been told that the building was haunted saw two dark figures studying an exhibition of items that had belonged to Parmly and his father. The taller figure appeared to be male and wore Victorian-era clothing, while the other was less distinct. They faded away before the startled intern could get a closer look.

In December 2003 another ghost made its presence known. One of the staff went to the basement early in the morning before the building was open to the public, and saw an elderly man sitting in one of the armchairs near the fireplace. Not long after, the same ghost was seen again, this time by two young interns who hadn't known of the first sighting.

Ghostly activity continues. A local medium states that the Western Heritage Center is home to many ghosts. According to her, one of them is a former librarian who worked there in 1918, but the majority of the ghosts are just "drop-ins," coming and going as they please.

Employees at the Western Heritage Center take it in stride—and wait with considerable interest to see what might happen next.

The Western Heritage Center welcomes visitors and offers a changing menu of exhibits relating to life in the West. Check out the toilets in the basement—two Cub Scouts who used the facilities claimed that someone rattled the doors of their stalls. When they looked to see who it was, no one was there. Perhaps "Priscilla" was in a mischievous mood that day!

THE GHOSTLY TRAIN CONDUCTOR

UNION DEPOT
Montana Avenue at 23rd Street
Billings, Montana
406-656-7273

Ghostly Activity Level: Low

HISTORY: The Union Depot is a complex of sand-colored brick buildings. It was called "union" because at one time the facilities were shared by three railroad companies: the Northern Pacific, the Great Northern, and the Chicago, Burlington & Quincy. Abandoned when AMTRAK discontinued passenger service across southern Montana in 1979, the depot has since been purchased by the city of Billings and renovated. It is occasionally open for special events.

PHENOMENA: During filming of a motion picture in the old passenger terminal in 1991, buckets of paint mysteriously tipped over and members of the film crew saw an apparition wearing an old-fashioned conductor's uniform and cap. More recently, odd reflections have turned up on photos taken by a professional photographer doing a fashion shoot in the terminal. Employees at the Beanery Bar and Grill, located in the complex, have heard a phantom voice calling their names.

The Union Depot is the fourth railroad depot to have served Billings since 1882. The first was abandoned after a year because it was too far from the fledgling business district. The second was in Headquarters Hotel, hastily thrown up by the railroad to house its engineers during construction of the rail line. The ramshackle structure soon became an eyesore; it burned down in 1891, helped by firemen and onlookers who enthusiastically tossed everything from mattresses to lanterns onto the blaze just to make sure nothing would be left of the hotel.

Next was a brick depot on North 28th Street, but that one soon proved too small to handle the increased freight and passenger traffic. The existing Union Depot was built around 1909 and handled passenger traffic until 1979. Abandoned, the depot fell prey to vandals and vagrants who occasionally broke in to bed down inside the formerly splendid passenger terminal. Word got around on the streets that the depot was a spooky place to be at night. Whispering voices were heard and shadowy figures were glimpsed. At the time, the tales were dismissed as nothing more than alcohol-induced hallucinations.

In 1991, director Ron Howard decided to film parts of "Far and Away," starring Tom Cruise and Nicole Kidman, at the old depot. By then the buildings were in deplorable condition. The film company cleaned up the property, replaced broken windows, and restored the passenger terminal to the way it would have looked around 1900. Hundreds of local people were hired as extras.

It wasn't long before odd things began to happen. The late Richard "Taz" Worden, a retired private investigator who acted in the film, told me that on a hot July day the temperature inside the building suddenly plummeted. The cold became so intense that the film crew had to open the doors to let in warm air. On another occasion, the crew watched in disbelief as buckets of crackle paint left alone on a scaffold tipped over one by one.

Whispering voices were heard coming from an empty corner, just as vagrants had reported in the early 1980s. The voices were quite distinct and obviously those of several men, but the words could not be made out. And sometimes the sounds of men working were heard from the east end of the terminal when no one was at that end of the building.

During the filming of the big fight scene in the passenger terminal, Worden and three other actors saw a man wearing a conductor's hat and uniform, complete with a railroad watch on a chain, walk down the tunnel toward the baggage room. They knew that no one in the cast matched his description, so they quickly followed him into the baggage room. No one was there.

In 1997 a professional photographer had an interesting experience while shooting publicity photos in the baggage room. When her film was developed, there were odd reflections on the photos where there should have been none. She had never had this happen to her before. She also stated that everyone in her group felt uneasy in the building, and no one wanted to linger once the shooting was done.

Strong emotion seems to be one of the keys to a haunting, and no doubt countless heartbreaking departures as well as joyous reunions have occurred in the passenger terminal, particularly during World War I and World War II when troop trains stopped at Billings. Perhaps that emotion somehow has imprinted on the fabric of the building and can be sensed at times.

That theory would not explain the sudden intense cold that hindered the film crew, however, or the falling buckets of crackle paint. A local railroad enthusiast told me he had heard that, not long after the terminal was built, a ticket agent was accidentally shot and killed by a cowboy who wanted to buy a ticket. While reaching for his wallet, the cowboy somehow had dislodged his pistol from its holster. The pistol struck the counter, discharged, and killed the clerk. Could the actors who saw the figure walk into the baggage room have mistaken a ticket agent's uniform for that of a conductor? It's certainly possible. So far my search of newspaper microfilm hasn't turned up an article about a shooting at the depot, but perhaps someday a researcher will be able to verify the story.

The renovated depot now is part of an ambitious project involving the downtown historic district. The passenger terminal is occasionally rented for weddings and other special occasions. Recently, men working alone in the building heard chairs scraping across the floor in the caterer's office. When they investigated, they found that several chairs had been moved from their usual places. Perhaps the ghost of the clerk was trying to tidy up his office space.

The Beanery also is haunted. The structure has been remodeled and the only original parts remaining are the windows and the wall tiles in the kitchen. If ghosts cling to the physical fabric of buildings they knew in life, they wouldn't find much left here.

I stopped in for a sandwich and a bowl of their famous bean soup just before Christmas. As I stood waiting to pay for lunch, I felt something, a touch of icy air hovering just behind me. On a hunch, I asked the cashier, "Do you have any old railroad ghosts here?"

He looked surprised, then nodded. He and eight or nine other employees had experienced some strange happenings in the building. Occasionally they would hear their names called. "It sounds loud," the cashier said, "but as if it's coming from around a corner." There is never anyone there when they go to look. Sometimes pots or pans are lifted from their hooks and flung across the kitchen. Scalding hot water occasionally is found running, even though the taps had been shut off.

Who is the ghost of the Beanery? The story is that a man came to the depot one day to meet his sweetheart, who was supposed to arrive on a particular train. She didn't show up. He returned every day for years to greet the trains, but she never arrived. He is said to have eventually died of a broken heart.

Oddly enough, I found an article in the August 26, 1902 *Billings Gazette* about a man who actually did meet the trains every day for weeks, waiting for his fiancée to arrive. She had been unavoidably detained by a death in her family, but finally arrived a month late. The depot in question was an earlier building on North 28th Street, though, so it's hard to know whether a folk memory of an actual event has been transferred to the present depot or whether the ghost of the Beanery is unrelated. Perhaps time will tell.

Keep your eyes and ears open when you visit the renovated passenger terminal. Perhaps you'll hear a ghostly whisper or catch a glimpse of the phantom conductor striding along with an eye on his watch. And do stop at the Beanery for a great sandwich or a bowl of bean soup made from the original railroad recipe. You may get more than is on the menu. I've rated the ghostly activity level at the depot as low because it's open so seldom, but the Beanery's activity level probably rates at least a "moderate."

MURRAY'S
CLOSET

JULIANO'S RESTAURANT
2912 7th Avenue North
Billings, Montana 59101
406-248-6400

Ghostly Activity Level: Moderate

HISTORY: The house currently occupied by Juliano's Restaurant first appears in city directories in 1920, but it may have been built earlier as the carriage house for a nearby mansion. The house was occupied for many years by Ernest E. Murray, an accountant, and his wife Amy. After they died the house changed hands several times before award-winning chef Carl Kurokawa and two partners bought it in 1995.

PHENOMENA: Workers have seen a ghostly figure on the stairs. A closet door in "Murray's Room" mysteriously opens by itself. A wine glass broke for no apparent reason when employees discussed the ghost. The clatter of a dog's claws has been heard where there was no dog, and at least two diners have encountered moving cold spots.

I first heard about a possible haunting at Juliano's from a passenger on the "Haunted Historic Billings" trolley tour. She had witnessed poltergeist activity at the restaurant, with plates and other objects flying off shelves. Not long after, on a cold March day in 1999, I decided to visit Juliano's with my ghosthunting partner Pat Cody. Chef Carl Kurokawa had agreed to take a few minutes from his busy schedule to sit down with us in the haunted "Murray's Room" and tell us about his experiences with the ghost.

Kurokawa, a tall, imposing figure, came to Billings in 1980 from his home state of Hawaii, where he had worked in numerous restaurants on several islands. After working as executive chef for the Radisson Northern Hotel and DeVerniero's Ristorante in Billings, he decided to open his own restaurant and began to search for a suitable building near downtown.

Kurokawa told us that when he was considering buying the place, the owner informed him that the building was haunted by a ghost she called "Murray," after the original owner. She claimed that the closet door in "Murray's Room" on the second floor sometimes opened by itself, and whenever it did, odd things happened. Kurokawa didn't take the stories seriously and bought the house.

During the renovation, however, workers complained that someone would come up behind them and stand there watching. Whenever they turned around to see who it was, no one was there. Occasionally a worker would put down a tool for a moment, only to find the tool missing or moved the next time he reached for it. One worker even thought he saw a man's figure on the stairs, but the image wasn't clear enough to identify.

On a warm evening during the remodeling, Kurokawa came back to the restaurant at dusk to make sure the compressors were running. The compressors were located upstairs, next to Murray's Room. Dusk provided just enough light for

Kurokawa to see his way without turning on the house lights. He let himself into the silent building and started up the stairs. When he reached the landing he suddenly recalled the previous owner's tales about the closet door that sometimes opened by itself.

Murray's Room loomed just ahead, with the compressor in a room farther along the corridor. Kurokawa knew the closet door had been closed when he'd left earlier that day. Would it still be closed?

As he neared the room, he put up one hand to shield his eyes. *Don't let the closet door be open,* he thought to himself. *PLEASE don't let the closet door be open.* As he passed the doorway to Murray's Room he couldn't resist a quick glance inside. The closet door stood wide open! Kurokawa quickly checked the compressors and left the building.

Some of Kurokawa's employees also have had odd experiences. Two of the waitresses told me that objects sometimes moved by themselves. One of the waiters agreed. One day the young man had been talking about the ghost with several other employees just before the restaurant opened for lunch. He poured some Pepsi into a wine glass and had just set it down when the bowl neatly separated itself from the stem and tipped over.

"Things do seem to happen more when we talk about the ghost," he acknowledged. "Especially if someone's skeptical."

Although the ghost's features have never been clearly seen, everyone agrees it's a man. The most likely candidate is Ernest Murray, who lived there with his wife for many years. Just why Murray should take a special interest in the upstairs closet is unknown, but the closet door has been found open many times, and ghostly activity usually follows.

Many older homes have uneven floors, and sometimes the doorframes have sagged. Could that be the answer to a door that apparently opens by itself? I examined the floor carefully. It appeared to be level, and the closet door fit snugly in its frame. I turned the old-fashioned doorknob and found that it took a determined effort to open the door. There didn't appear to be any way that the door could swing open by itself.

Pat and I took a number of photos and decided to return that evening for dinner. We were seated at a table in a corner of the main dining room near the entrance to the kitchen. As we glanced over the menus, we both heard the distinct sound of dog claws scrabbling on the wood floor in front of the kitchen door. We each own a dog, and automatically turned to see what kind of dog it was. There was no dog, and the floor in front of the kitchen door was empty. We questioned our waitress, but none of the staff had previously encountered a ghostly dog at Juliano's.

About 20 minutes later we were enjoying our dinner when we felt someone walk up to our table. At the same time, a wave of frigid air engulfed us. We looked up, startled, but no one was visible. I was seated next to a hot radiator, and until then our corner had been almost too warm. One of the phenomena often said to occur in haunted places is an unexplained and sudden drop in temperature, so I decided to try an experiment. I stretched out my arm, right through the frigid mass, to see how far it extended. It seemed to be about the diameter of a human body. I could wiggle my fingers in comfortably warm air just beyond the icy pillar. After about 30 seconds the temperature returned to normal and we no longer had the feeling of being watched by someone we couldn't see.

The entrance door was on the other side of the wall from

where we were sitting. Pat got up to see whether someone had opened the door, letting in cold night air, and came back shaking her head. No one had entered or left the restaurant. There seemed to be no explanation for the icy column of air that had swept up to our table.

Does the spirit of Ernest Murray haunt Juliano's? So far, the ghost hasn't been seen clearly enough to be identified. Whoever he is, he has made his presence known to the former owner, several workers, a noted chef and many of his staff, the lady on the trolley, and Pat and me. He also may be responsible for the light on the upper floor that was seen after midnight by a passing security guard, who checked and found an empty building.

Perhaps Murray is pleased that Carl Kurokawa and his partners have restored the building so beautifully, or perhaps he's merely curious about the visitors who come and go in his old home. In any case, his unearthly presence lends added charm to an already distinguished restaurant.

Visit Juliano's to enjoy both an excellent meal and the restaurant's turn-of-the-century ambiance. Be sure to visit Murray's Room upstairs. And don't forget to offer a friendly greeting to the ghost of Ernest Murray—just in case.

GHOSTS IN
THE LIBRARY

PARMLY BILLINGS LIBRARY
510 North Broadway
Billings, Montana 59101
406-657-8258

Activity level: High

HISTORY: The original Parmly Billings Library opened in 1901, the gift of the family of railroad magnate Frederick Billings. Named for Billings' deceased son Parmly, the library soon became a social center for the rapidly expanding town. In 1969 the library moved to larger quarters in the former Billings Hardware building. The Sanborn Fire Map of 1912 shows Partington's Greenhouses taking up most of the site of the present library building. By the 1930s, the greenhouse was gone and a number of private residences and small businesses had been built on the property. In 1955, they were torn down to make way for the huge Billings Hardware store. Both the old library building, now the Western Heritage Center, and the current library building are haunted. Perhaps some of the ghosts once lived or worked in one of the buildings that previously stood on the site.

PHENOMENA: The ghost of a dark-haired woman is seen in the basement of the present library building. A ghost man wearing jeans and work boots made an appearance on the second floor early one morning. A security guard and an employee both saw a white "something" cross the roof outside the fifth-floor windows. Stairwell doors slam shut even though no one has opened them. A library patron saw someone move past her in the Montana Room, but no one was there when she turned to see who it was. A security guard once walked through a foggy cloud that hovered in the stairwell between the garage and the mezzanine.

Many libraries are haunted. It's almost a tradition to have a resident ghost, just as it is in the theater world. Some library ghosts are former staff members apparently still conscientiously going about their duties, while the others may just find libraries a comfortable place in which to spend at least a part of their afterlife.

When I began working at Parmly Billings Library in 1986, I heard rumors that the basement was haunted. Odd noises were heard that couldn't be blamed on the heating and ventilating equipment. Light cords would swing wildly. Once or twice, staff members who worked in the basement reported feeling watched. I often went to the basement to fetch books for patrons, but years passed without anything unusual happening, and eventually I forgot the rumors.

One Saturday morning in 1998 I took the elevator to the basement to fetch a book from storage. The library had not yet opened, so only employees were in the building—or so I assumed. As the elevator doors opened, however, I saw someone dart across the end of the aisle ahead of me and disappear into the book stacks. I had the impression that it was a young male, but it moved so quickly I couldn't be sure. It looked solid, completely gray in color.

For a moment I debated hurrying after the intruder, but

common sense prevailed. I took the elevator back to the first floor and summoned our security guard. He and I searched the entire basement thoroughly and found no one.

Then I recalled the uncanny silence of that figure. If the intruder had been human, I should have heard running footsteps on the concrete floor. And how had he gotten into the building without setting off the alarms? It seemed that I had finally seen the rumored ghost.

It quickly became apparent that he wasn't the only ghost. On a summer afternoon in 2003, employee Deb Jennings went to the basement. She had just put her hand on a book when she saw a movement from the corner of her eye. Peering around the corner of the book stack was a woman with dark hair parted in the middle. She seemed to be crouching down, as if hoping to remain unseen.

Deb and the woman locked eyes, and Deb felt the hair stand up on her head. The woman wasn't one of the staff, and no one else could have gotten into the basement without a key. Deb broke eye contact and walked very quickly to the elevator. She felt the woman following her, but refused to look around. Once safely in the elevator, she quickly punched the button for the first floor, not taking her eyes off the control panel until the doors closed.

"I knew she was standing by the door," Deb told me later. "I didn't want to see her."

Deb, the security guard, and two other staff members immediately went back down and searched the basement, but found no one.

Who was the stranger? Perhaps the same woman seen on the third floor the same year by Ray Ostrum, a maintenance man. He described her as medium height with shoulder-length brown hair, in her late 30s or early 40s, wearing glasses. Ray saw her through the windows of one of the meeting rooms on the third floor and assumed she was a real person, perhaps looking for someone. She had vanished by the time he reached the door to ask whether he could assist her. Ray also has heard a woman's laughter on two occasions while he was cleaning the third floor. No one else was present on either occasion.

What Ray didn't know was that my video camera had picked up a woman's laughter one Saturday morning on the third floor. I had set up a tape recorder and a video camera to see whether anything odd would happen. When I came back at lunchtime, I discovered that the tape recorder had been turned off. There was plenty of tape left and the batteries were fresh. Annoyed, I turned it back on and spoke aloud to the ghost: "Well, it's obvious you don't want to make your presence known on cassette." When I played back the videotape, a woman's laugh could be heard when I spoke aloud to the ghost.

Ghostly activity also occurred on the second floor, where library volunteer Chase Nottingham had a strange experience in December 2003. Chase had been a military policeman for eleven years and was a trained observer. He had come to work at six-thirty that morning. It was still dark outside, so he went over to the light panel and turned on the lights. "When I started back," he told me, "I noticed that the lights in the northeast corner were still out. I saw a dim figure, silhouetted by lights outside the windows, appear to the right of the bookcase in that corner. It turned slightly and stepped behind the row of books, then stepped back out.

"The skin of my arms, neck, and face tingled. I didn't challenge the figure, but observed it for fifteen to twenty seconds. It appeared to be a male Caucasian, five-feet-ten to six feet, of slight to average build, perhaps one-hundred-sixty pounds. What hair I saw was short, dark blonde to light brown.

A squared black or dark hat with a short bill was on his head. His jacket or heavy shirt was black or dark, with shortened sleeves so both wrists and hands showed. His trousers were also dark, the cuffs high enough to show ankles and brogans below.

"I returned to the light panel and flipped on the last two switches. I was gone no longer than five seconds. The lights in the area where the figure had appeared had come on, and it was no longer in sight. I walked to the aisle in the corner. As I approached, the tingling increased, and the hairs on my arms and nape of my neck stood up.

"No one was in any of the aisles I passed. However, an armchair had been moved from its place approximately where the figure had stood to the far northeast corner of second floor. The vinyl seat of the chair was cold to my touch. A round library stepstool was in front of the chair, as if used as an ottoman. A stack of a dozen or so books was beside them. A musky odor reminiscent of sawdust hung strongly in the area. I made a rapid but thorough search of second floor, keeping the spiral stairway and elevator in sight. I returned the displaced chair to its usual place and put the stack of books on a table. By then the odor had vanished, as had my tingling and literal hair-raising."

Long-time security officer Dan Damjanovich saw something even odder on the fifth floor. He had gone up to the staff lunchroom on break and was talking to his wife on the phone when a tall, thin shape moved past the windows overlooking the room. It resembled a person dressed in white. "I have to go," Damjanovich told his wife. "Someone's out on the roof!" He bolted onto the roof in pursuit. No one was there, nor had anyone gone down the stairway that led from the roof to the garage. Whatever it was had vanished.

In 2005, a new employee had an unnerving experience on

the fifth floor while taking a break. She looked up from the book she was reading in time to see a man come into the room from the kitchen. He was well over six feet, and looked like a figure made of smoked glass. The moment he realized she could see him, he turned and went back into the kitchen. The employee expected to hear the door open from the kitchen out onto the roof, but there was no sound. She cautiously went into the kitchen, but no one was there and the door was still closed.

In the autumn of 2005, construction crews began to bring the library building up to current fire codes. They worked mostly at night, and it wasn't long before odd things began to happen. Mike Williams, construction supervisor and master carpenter, had grown up in a haunted house and the phenomena didn't particularly bother him. "The first thing I recall was the whistling on second floor," he told me. "I was getting ready to frame the wall near the south wall at the time. The whistling wasn't real close, but it was definitely in the room. I thought someone had come in, so I turned on all the lights and took a tour, but didn't find anyone. It was kind of like a two-note whistle, like someone was trying to get my attention. I heard it twice."

"That same night," he continued, "I went downstairs to get things I needed to frame the wall, and went back up on the freight elevator. I found a chair pulled out from one of the tables. I pushed it back, set the sheetrock up, went back downstairs for a vacuum, and when I came back up I found a different chair pulled out. It was set at an angle like someone was sitting there watching me work.

Another time I was working in the staff break room on fifth floor. I was up on a ladder. Two of the staff were there too, both sitting down. Out of the corner of my eye I saw someone walk past me, open the door onto the roof, and go out. I heard the door close. I thought one of the staff had just got up and left, but they were both still there. The person I saw was about seven feet tall."

The construction crew had not been told about the odd things that had happened in the building over the years, and Williams would have had no way of knowing that a staff member had seen a very tall apparition on the fifth floor just a few weeks earlier.

That wasn't all he experienced. "One night I went down to the basement on the freight elevator. I felt something get in the elevator with me. The hair just stood up on my head. When the elevator door opened on the third floor, the feeling went away. I told the other guys that 'Fred' just rode up with me.

"I was touched, too, while working alone one night on the second floor. I had just sheetrocked and insulated the old dumbwaiter, and I had my hand on the measuring tape clipped to my belt. I felt something touch my hand. I looked to see if a spider was there, but there was nothing. Later I felt pressure as something grabbed my hand. It didn't feel like distinct fingers, just pressure."

Other crew members also had unnerving experiences. Two of the men heard whistling in the basement. They couldn't tell where it was coming from. A painter working on the third floor heard someone walk up behind him on two occasions. Both times he stood up and asked, "Is anyone here?" No one answered. The alarm on the third floor went off one night, indicating a water leak, but no leak was found. The motion detectors on the third floor also tripped when no one was working on that floor. Mike Williams and his crew went there, looking for an invader, but found no one. They reset the detectors but it happened again not long afterward. Again, no one was found.

The most alarming occurrence happened one night when Mike Williams started down the stairs from the mezzanine to the first floor. When he reached the door, he felt his hair stand on end. "I saw a dark, swirling fog," he said. "I decided it wasn't a good idea to go through that doorway. After that, I stopped working alone at night."

In March 2006 workmen returned once more to the library. Construction appears to stir up ghostly activity, so we waited to see if anything would happen. On a Saturday morning one of our staff got on the elevator to take a cart of books up to the second floor. The library had not yet opened for business and the elevator was locked. As she flicked the switch to turn it on, she heard a male voice say crossly from overhead, "Well, here we (expletive) go again!"

We'll probably never know just who the young man in gray was, or the older man in work boots on second floor, or the dark-haired woman in the basement, or why they choose to make their presence known to the living at times. Perhaps it's just that they have discovered that libraries are quiet, friendly places that welcome everyone—even ghosts.

If you visit, try sitting quietly in the Montana Room for an hour or so. A number of people have caught a glimpse of movement in the book stacks nearby, but when they look up, no one is there. And if the elevator door should open by itself when you approach with an armful of books, don't worry—it's probably just an obliging ghost.

CASA SANCHEZ

CASA SANCHEZ
719 South 9th Avenue
Bozeman, Montana 59715
406-586-4516

Ghostly Activity Level: Low

HISTORY: The Casa Sanchez was established in 1980 by the Sanchez family, who still own and operate the restaurant. The building was formerly a private home, built around 1895. One of the former owners of the house was rumored to have died in his bedroom of natural causes sometime around 1936.

PHENOMENA: On rare occasions, the figure of an old man is seen walking toward today's bathrooms, where his bedroom previously was located. Unexplained noises are sometimes heard from the basement around one o'clock in the morning.

One of the best Mexican restaurants in Montana is located near the Montana State University campus in Bozeman. A possible haunting at the restaurant was first brought to my attention by a former employee, Kels Koch, who encountered the ghost in 1988.

Koch said, "I worked at Casa Sanchez from December

1986 until September of 1989. It was started in 1980 by the brother-and-sister team of Ron and Gail Sanchez. I was friends with Ron, from the campus radio station KGLT. We used to go out and listen to bands, as I was in a pretty popular band at the time, the Beat Nothings, and Ron was a big music fan who started playing a year or two later.

"After my first year or so of working at the restaurant, Ron and Gail both felt comfortable letting me close up the place on nights they had to leave early. I was the last one out on that particular night. The waitress, hostess, dishwasher, and prep cook had already taken off for the night. I was just a few minutes behind them, because I had to put a roast in overnight to slow cook—something we did every few nights to supply us with the beef for our dishes.

"As I was wrapping the pan in foil, out of the corner of my eye I saw someone walk by the entrance into the kitchen. I was used to seeing people walk by that spot dozens of times a day, on their way to one of the bathrooms or, during the summer, to the backyard where we also served food in good weather. Well, after a second, I just shook my head and chuckled, remembering that I was the last person in the building and therefore *couldn't* have seen anyone!

"I thought it was just a flash of light or something—perhaps some car lights coming through the window of the side door that led into the kitchen, so I put it out of my head, finished wrapping the roast and put it in the oven, and took off into the Bozeman night.

"The next day I was working with Gail and just happened to mention that, for a second, I could have sworn I saw someone walk by as I was preparing the roast the previous night. She said very matter-of-factly, 'Oh yeah, we have a ghost.'

"Gail then went on to tell me that the building had once been a house, and the patriarch of the family had his bedroom in what was now the women's bathroom. If I remember the story correctly, he died in his bedroom sometime around 1936.

"Ever since she told me this story, I've always believed that I somehow looked through a window in time and saw the old man walk into 'his' room! That was it. There was no sound or drop in temperature, just a split-second vision that was almost subliminal. It wasn't scary or eerie, and I certainly didn't feel threatened. I just thought my eyes were playing a trick on me. Since I hadn't previously known of the spirit, however, it couldn't have been anything I imagined. Over the year and a half that I remained at the restaurant, neither I nor anyone else saw or heard from the old man—at least not that I ever heard of."

What could be more irresistible to a ghost hunter than a restaurant offering tasty Mexican cuisine plus the chance of a ghostly encounter for dessert? Frank, Sue, and I stopped in for lunch. The house was painted a bright yellow that glowed, despite the overcast autumn day. There are three dining rooms on the main floor, plus the kitchen and bathrooms. Stairs lead up to a private apartment.

We arrived a few minutes ahead of the lunch crowd, so I asked our waitress about the ghost. She replied quite matter-of-factly that she hadn't seen it, but she had heard footsteps going up the stairs when no one was on the stairs. A few minutes later, manager Michael Keyshae came over to talk with us. Keyshae and his wife, Lori (née Sanchez), have owned the restaurant for eight years.

"I used to think we had someone going up the stairs at nine o'clock at night, but I figured out that when the cleaner was working, whenever they'd bump something it would make noises like someone was going up the stairs," he answered when we asked about the ghost.

I must have looked a bit disappointed, because he added, "We also hear strange noises in the basement about one A.M. We never have figured out what causes the noises, and the servers are afraid to go down there." Our waitress acknowledged that the basement felt "creepy" to her, even though it appeared quite ordinary.

I asked Keyshae whether there had been anything unusual about the former owner's death. "As far as I know," he replied, "he died in his room of natural causes. Back then, of course, most people died at home."

Apparently the people who used to live in the house before the Sanchez family bought it never noticed anything unusual. Keyshae said they come to the restaurant once or twice a year and reminisce about what a great house it was in which to live.

Keyshae offered to let us try the house specialty, a drink called Hot Rocks. It consists of hot pepper juice frozen into miniature ice cubes that are dropped into a glass of 7UP. I was a little hesitant at first, but pleasantly surprised to find it tasted a bit like lemonade. As the ice cubes melted, the concentration of pepper juice increased and the drink got hotter. It was a wonderfully warming drink for cold weather.

Another house specialty, probably unique to the Casa Sanchez, is a whole bowl of whipped cream for children or adults, with your choice of chocolate sauce or hot fudge on top. I managed to resist the temptation to order it on that visit but will definitely try it on the next. After all, ghost hunting does take a lot of energy!

Sue and I decided to look at the ladies' bathroom, located in the former owner's bedroom. I picked up nothing unusual on either audiotape or film. Perhaps what Kels Koch had seen that night in 1988 was not a spirit but what is called a "place memory," a sort of replay of an activity that has taken place many times in the past. Or perhaps the ghost of the elderly owner had, with old-fashioned courtesy, simply left when I walked in. If so, I wonder what he makes of the steady stream of strangers who walk into what he probably still views as his bedroom?

You may want to arrive a little early for lunch or supper to avoid the crowds. And be sure to try the Hot Rocks. If you happen to catch a glimpse of an elderly gentleman walking down the hall toward the bathrooms at the rear of the main floor, consider yourself fortunate—you've just seen the former owner of the house.

STRAND UNION THEATER

STRAND UNION THEATER
Department of Media & Theater Arts
Montana State University
Bozeman, Montana 59717
406-994-2484

Ghostly Activity Level: Low

HISTORY: The Strand Union Building, originally the university's Student Union Building, was constructed in 1940 during a period of rapid expansion on campus. In the mid-1950s, professor Joseph C. Fitch, dynamic head of the Theater Arts department, began to campaign for a theater. When the Student Union Building was renovated, the Strand Union Theater was carved into what had been a large ballroom. The first play produced in the new theater was *Rainmaker*, in January 1957.

PHENOMENA: Footsteps are heard going up or down a spiral metal staircase that leads from a room behind the stage to the lower levels. A man resembling Professor Fitch has been seen in the sound booth, and a female ghost wearing a ball gown from the 1920s is reputed to haunt the auditorium, once part of the ballroom. In one of the rooms below the stage, another female ghost wearing clothes from the early nineteenth century left a scent of lavender perfume and scrawled notes pleading for help.

Many college campuses are reputed to be haunted. The stories usually involve a supposed suicide or murder, although very few can be traced to an actual event. Here in Montana, ghost stories are told of Carroll College in Helena, the University of Montana–Missoula, Montana State University–Billings, and Rocky Mountain College in Billings. Not to be outdone, the Strand Union Theater at Montana State University–Bozeman is reputed to be haunted by at least two spirits, one of them a former faculty member.

In November 1974, Professor Joseph C. Fitch, director of the university's theater arts program for nearly 20 years, slipped while descending the spiral staircase that leads from an area immediately behind the stage to a room on the lower level. He suffered a severe concussion and, according to those who worked with him at the time, never fully recovered from the effects of the fall. On November 22, 1974, he committed suicide in his office with a prop gun. Fitch's strong personality, talent, and dedication to the theater have led many to conclude that at least some of the phenomena said to occur in the 50-year-old theater can be attributed to his restless spirit.

Stories of a haunting were circulating well before his tragic death. Apparently a young woman wearing a ball gown was seen in the theater (once part of the ballroom) as far back as the late 1960s. It's thought that she had committed suicide by hanging herself in the ballroom. However, when Debra Munn, author of *Big Sky Ghosts,* contacted long-time employees, none of them could recall any such incident. In addition, the ghost's gown was described as dating from the late 1920s or early 1930s, and the Student Union Building was not built until 1940. Despite the discrepancies, eyewitnesses remain convinced that the ghost of a woman in old-fashioned evening dress has haunted the theater for many years.

I had arrived at the Strand Union Theater half an hour early for my appointment with a representative of the Media and Theater Arts Department. While my friends Frank and Sue wandered around the auditorium, snapping photos at random to see if anything unusual would turn up on film, I approached the half-dozen students who were constructing a set on stage. I explained that I was looking for ghost stories on campus and asked whether any of them had ever experienced anything odd in the theater. They all shook their heads no.

"A girl I knew said she had," one young woman offered tentatively. "She graduated a couple of years ago. She said that once she was up on the catwalk and saw something." And that was all she recalled. Everyone in the group was aware of the stories, but apparently there had been no recent ghostly activity.

Just then the professor arrived for our meeting. He prefers to remain anonymous, citing all the phone calls he gets whenever he's quoted in newspaper articles. "Professor X" has worked in the Media and Theater Arts Department for 30 years. He doesn't believe the theater is haunted, pointing out that actors are trained to use their imaginations.

I asked him whether he considered himself a skeptic. His answer surprised me. "I'm actually a believer in ghosts," he said. "At least I believe there are people who can see ghosts."

Has he ever had any strange experiences in the theater?

"Well," he answered, "when you come to a place and there are ghost stories about a place, you kind of get that in your head somehow. One time I was in my office, about two o'clock in the morning. I'd been working all day long on some drafting and I just got to thinking about ghosts. All of a sudden I felt uncomfortable. I never saw anything, I never felt anything. I never smelled any strange smells or heard bumps in the night. I just left. It was time to go home anyway."

What about the stories that two students had seen the ghost of Joe Fitch in the sound booth?

Professor X was dismissive. "It would be very difficult to discern anything in the sound room," he said. "Even when the lights are on in there, it's pretty dim."

He then led us backstage to where Professor Fitch's accident had occurred: a steep, narrow, iron, spiral staircase that led to a room beneath the stage. I followed Professor X down the stairs, carefully holding both railings. It was easy to see how a moment of inattention could lead to a bad fall. Apparently Professor Fitch had slipped near the top and tumbled all the way to the bottom.

We followed Professor X through a doorway to the costume storage area. "A student was actually living here for a while," he told us. "She was working in our costume shop, and had set up a cot in the alcove here. She apparently was leaving notes and someone was responding, writing things like 'Help me!' She said she sometimes smelled a lavender perfume, too."

Warming to the subject, he continued, "Another girl was working in the costume shop. When she came upstairs one day, all the power tools in the shop turned on at the same time. Now this building is old and the electricity is whacky. We have power surges, that kind of thing, quirky wiring. It was odd, though."

One play seemed to provoke ghostly activity, according to Professor X: "One of them was *Damn Yankees*. Neil Hirsig, one of the faculty, was playing the part of the devil. He swore that someone grabbed his ankles and tripped him when he was going down some stairs on the set."

Professor Gerry Roe, now head of the Theater Arts department at Rocky Mountain College, was a faculty member at MSU–Bozeman from 1981 to 1989, based in Professor Fitch's old office. He didn't hesitate to acknowledge that he'd had two odd experiences while at MSU.

"One incident involved the son of a faculty member," he said. "He was just a little kid. One day he happened to be in my office, crawling on the floor, drawing on a big piece of paper. He was using a red magic marker. When he left, I picked up the paper. There on the floor was the outline in red magic marker of a body. I brought his father in, and he said 'Yes, that's where he [Professor Fitch] was.' It wasn't solid but it was enough of an outline to see the body. The kid wasn't drawing that, he was moving the paper all around. That's what's so weird about it.

"The other incident also happened in the office. In theater we end up being here really late at night, whether we want to be or not. One night I was in there and I had a desk lamp on. I had to get some work done and I looked up and I swear to God there was a person standing there. The office door was locked. I thought, 'Oh, I'm not going to believe that,' so I went back to writing. When I looked up again, there wasn't a person there. I thought, 'I'm going home now, this isn't that important.'

"He had a real rustic look to him, very rustic. We were doing a play called *Annie Get Your Gun*. It was just odd. He had a hat on, the brim down a bit. He was clean-shaven, but not in well-kept clothes. There was a downtrodden feeling to it. I wondered if my mind was playing tricks with the characters in the play. I reviewed all the characters in the play but there was no character like him.

"He kind of stood there. He wasn't frowning, wasn't smiling. I didn't feel frightened or anything. He was standing right in front of me. He was in shades of gray. I remember thinking to myself that he looked sick. I looked down at my papers and when I looked up again he was gone.

"Another time, a student in a show I was directing said she had seen a face in the lighting booth, and she took off running. I don't know if it was a ghost or a student in the lighting booth. We stayed another ten minutes and then we all left as a group."

Despite a campaign to save it, the Strand Union Theater was closed in 2007 and scheduled for demolition. A new "black box" theater will be built nearby. If ghosts are no more than emotional energies that have been absorbed by their surroundings, the haunting will probably cease once the old theater has been destroyed. On the other hand, if there is an actual spirit present, it may or may not attach itself to the new theater. Only time will tell.

THE
GUARDIANS

HIGHWAY 464 (DUCK LAKE ROAD)
Browning to Babb, Montana

Ghostly Activity Level: Low

HISTORY: Duck Lake, on the Blackfeet Indian Reservation, is widely regarded as one of the best trout fisheries in Montana. It has been stocked with trout for almost a century, and managed by the tribe since the 1950s. Duck Lake Road, now Montana Highway 464, runs in a wide curve around the lake. It is heavily traveled in the summer months by anglers, and tourists on their way to Glacier National Park, and nearly deserted in winter.

PHENOMENA: At rare intervals, people who find themselves in trouble along this sparsely settled road have been aided by three mysterious men in a car. The occurrences seem to happen only during winter. Drivers have reported seeing oncoming headlights that vanish mysteriously, even though there is no place to turn off the road.

Russ Storey, former elementary school principal at Browning, related an eerie story told to him by a long-time friend and prominent citizen of Browning, who is now dead. "It was during the late 1920s or early 1930s that my friend, whom I will call 'John,' had an odd experience. Unmarried at the time, John decided to visit friends in Babb. He had an old car of unknown make and year and was anxious to travel. The road from Browning to Babb passed Duck Lake in a sweeping curve while climbing up and over a large hill. It was thirty miles from Browning to Babb.

"John was on this gravel road when a blizzard struck in full force, making visibility nearly zero. The swirling snow was quickly blown into drifts across the road. John was perhaps twelve miles from Browning when his car became trapped in a large drift. As he watched in horror, the drift continued to grow. After nearly an hour John began to fear for his safety, as he was thoroughly stuck and didn't know how far away he might be from one of the few houses along the road. He was reasonably comfortable as long as his car engine was running but was apprehensive about what would happen once he ran out of fuel.

"Just then he thought he noticed faint lights behind him. They grew in size and soon separated into the twin headlights of another vehicle. He wondered how anyone could possibly be traveling under these conditions, but rejoiced that he was no longer alone. When the vehicle pulled up to where his car was trapped, John jumped out and climbed over the drifts to the new vehicle, a late model car. There appeared to be three men inside. The driver opened his door and asked if there was any trouble. John explained that he was stuck and wanted to return to Browning. The driver said that he and his friends would be happy to help. The three men got out of their car, each of them carrying a shovel. None of them spoke as they worked to dig John's car out of the drift. When they had cleared enough of a path, they pushed as John backed out of the drift. John thought it strange that only the driver had talked, but he was too anxious to return home to take more careful note of the three men or their vehicle.

"The driver then told John that he would follow him to town to make sure he arrived safely. Slowly John drove back to Browning, with the reassuring headlights of his rescuers behind him. It seemed that the journey took a long time but at last John came over Houseman Hill and saw the welcoming lights of the community in front of him. The storm had abated and the strong winds were dying down. Just as John reached the edge of Browning, the headlights behind him suddenly vanished. John stopped his vehicle and stepped out of his car. Although he scanned his surroundings carefully, there was no sign of the other car. There were no houses in that area nor were there any cross roads onto which the car could have turned. There were no tracks in the snow except those made by the tires of his car.

"Until the day he died, John claimed he was rescued by guardian angels who, when their task of seeing him safely home was completed, disappeared, to reappear somewhere else in the world to provide service for another person in need. And although he told the story many times in later years, the details never varied."

"I myself have had some interesting experiences while driving that road during the winter months," Storey added. "It was nothing too exciting, just oncoming headlights that were seen at the top of a hill and then suddenly disappeared—when there was no place to turn off. I learned to take them pretty much for granted."

Are the headlights that mysteriously vanish those of the car driven by the three guardians, still patrolling the lonely road in case someone needs help? We'll probably never know for certain, but do keep your eyes open along Duck Lake Road. You may not see the three men, but the ghost of a Native American on a pony has reputedly been seen in this area as well.

THE ARTS
CHATEAU GHOST

ARTS CHATEAU MUSEUM
231 Broadway Street
Butte, Montana 59701
406-723-7600

Ghostly Activity Level: Moderate

HISTORY: The Charles Walker Clark Mansion was built in 1898 by "copper king" William Clark, as a wedding present for his eldest son Charles and his bride Catherine Quinn Roberts. The house may have been modeled after a French chateau the couple visited while honeymooning in Europe in 1896. The mansion later passed to the Murray family, who lived there from 1915 to 1945. One of the Murray's five sons died unexpectedly in the house and is thought to haunt it. The chateau now serves as a heritage museum and arts center.

PHENOMENA: A visitor reported seeing a female phantom. Cold spots on the stairs are detected by many people. Objects are sometimes moved, and footsteps often heard on the upper floors. Occasionally the motion detectors go off at night for no apparent reason, and one tour guide heard crashing chords on a piano when he was alone in the house.

Shawn Crowe, assistant to the director of the Butte-Silver

Bow Arts Foundation, had just begun to show us around the dining room on the second floor of the Arts Chateau Museum when he suddenly excused himself to hurry back downstairs. When he returned a few minutes later, he apologized and said, "I thought I heard the bell. That happens a lot, where the doorbell seems to ring." No one had been waiting on the doorstep and he hadn't seen anyone walking away, so he just chalked it up as another of the strange things that happen at the former home of Charles and Catherine Clark.

I hadn't heard the doorbell ring, nor anything else, except the soft shuffle of our feet as Shawn described the furnishings in the dining room. In fact, the mansion struck me as unnaturally silent, with none of the usual creaks or clicks of a building reacting to changes in temperature or wind.

I had arranged a private tour of the Arts Chateau Museum after reading an intriguing newspaper article by Roberta Stauffer entitled "Arts Chateau Ghost" in the Butte *Montana Standard* of August 15, 2001. According to the article, staff and visitors have reported some very odd goings-on at the mansion. One visitor claimed to have seen and spoken to a female ghost, while others felt cold spots on the stairway. A collection of puppets was found heaped in a pile one morning—although they had been carefully put away the day before—and motion detectors were reported to have gone off for no apparent reason. It sounded too good for a ghost hunter to resist, so I had arranged a private tour to check out the place myself.

I was surprised at how many modern conveniences the 108-year-old building had. The mansion was wired for electricity, a novelty at the time. Since then-unreliable electric power could go off for days or weeks, secondary sources of light included oil-burning wall sconces. A coal-fired furnace sent heat to radiators, and seven fireplaces added warmth and light. Modern plumbing added to the occupants' comfort.

The house was designed for entertaining, according to Crowe. Most of its owners were what would be described nowadays as jetsetters. Except for the Murrays, none had children. To discourage overnight guests, there were only two bedrooms among the twenty-seven rooms.

Reputedly the house was a replica of one of the wings of the French Chateau de Chenonceau, built to one-seventh scale. Although many of the rooms were good-sized, to me the ceilings seemed low and the rooms rather dark, possibly due to the reduced scale. Originally the house was decorated with an oriental motif, although most of that disappeared when the Murrays had it redecorated during their lengthy residence.

After touring the second and third floors, Frank, Sue, and I followed Shawn up the freestanding curved staircase to the fourth-floor ballroom, with its colorful Georgian hunting scenes on the walls. We took seats on a convenient bench while Shawn told us that in the early years, lavish entertainments were held in the ballroom and the state song, "Montana," was actually composed by one of the guests at a big party in 1908. Later, during the Murray occupancy, the ballroom was transformed into a dormitory for their five sons.

While Shawn was talking, I began to hear the faint strains of violins playing Strauss' "Tales from the Vienna Woods." At first I assumed the music was playing through a concealed sound system, but Frank and Sue were listening intently to Shawn and it was obvious that none of them noticed the music. Shawn didn't seem surprised when I told him about the music, though, for many visitors have sensed something uncanny on the fourth floor.

The music faded away a minute or two later. I wondered whether it might have had some connection with the female ghost seen by a visitor a few years earlier. Perhaps the ghostly lady had been a guest at the parties, or even the wife of one of the early owners, and was simply reliving happy memories. Of course, it may have been nothing more than imagination. I can only say that it seemed very real while it was happening, and that I couldn't seem to get the strains of the waltz out of my mind for quite a while afterward.

"Have you had any peculiar experiences in the building?" I asked Shawn.

"I've spent a lot of time alone here in the evenings," he replied, "but I hadn't experienced anything odd until last year. In January of every year we have a big wine-tasting festival. I was here by myself, cleaning on the third floor. It was in the middle of the day, and the building was locked up. All of a sudden, out of nowhere, I heard a big *bang bang* on a piano, like chords being struck. There's no rational explanation. If it had been a single 'ting' of a note, it could have been explained as a creak in the wood, but it was so obviously a couple of pounded chords. It seemed to come from the piano in the ballroom on the fourth floor, although it's hard to tell. I guess that it was John Murray letting me know he was here. Maybe I wasn't picking up on the small signals so he decided to give me something a little more obvious."

What about footsteps?

"Just since we've been walking around in here I thought I heard footsteps downstairs. I've always attributed them to the creak of an old building. Years ago the director of our foundation stayed here overnight for a few days, and he said he heard footsteps upstairs too.

"Other people have felt a slight push on the staircase, as if someone was trying to get past them, or a cold feeling. That's happened on more occasions than one. And once our director came in and found some china teacups set on edge in a way he couldn't duplicate. We blame it all on John Murray."

John was the second-oldest of the five boys. He died in the house on November 30, 1936, only 16 years old. According to family sources, he had come home early from football practice because he felt ill. He died the next day. He was remembered by classmates as friendly, a jokester, the type of person who might decide to play with a collection of puppets or balance teacups on edge just for fun.

We had enjoyed our tour, but it was time to head back to our hotel for the evening. Shawn lingered to shut off the ballroom lights while the three of us walked back to the stairway. I was in the lead, with Sue right behind me, and Frank trailing. I thought I'd try an experiment. "John?" I murmured as I neared the staircase, "Are you here? John Murray?" There was no answer. I hadn't really expected one. As I set my foot on the first step, however, I was suddenly engulfed by a mass of frigid air.

"It's icy cold at the head of the stairs," I called back to Shawn. Sue reached past my shoulder and nodded. She, too, could feel the frigid air. It lasted perhaps a few seconds before the temperature returned to normal.

"Is there an air return around here?" I asked Shawn when we were all safely at the bottom of the stairs, "Or anything that could cause a draft?"

He shook his head. "That's the main thing that people feel here, the most common experience people have in the building." We all glanced back at the stairway, now shrouded in shadows, and hastily started toward the front door, Shawn lingering just long enough to turn off the lights behind us. A few moments later he joined us outside. With the front door closed and securely locked, the Arts Chateau once more stood empty. Or did it?

The Charles Walker Clark Mansion gives visitors a fascinating look at the lives of those who had immense wealth early in the twentieth century. Perhaps you, too, will hear footsteps upstairs, or catch a glimpse of the female phantom reported by one visitor.

ROOKWOOD
SPEAKEASY

ROOKWOOD SPEAKEASY
Old Butte Historical Adventures
117 North Main Street
Butte, Montana 59701
406-498-3424

Ghostly Activity Level: Low

HISTORY: The Rookwood Hotel was built by James Pratt in 1912. The new 45-room hotel was one of the most elegant in Butte, featuring a marble entryway and a downstairs lobby in the European tradition. In 1950 the hotel was divided into apartments and named the LaSalle Apartments. A new owner began to restore the hotel in 2004. During the process of removing debris that had piled up for decades, a speakeasy dating from Prohibition Days was discovered hidden behind a bulletproof door in the basement.

PHENOMENA: The ghosts of two men wearing clothing from the 1920s have been seen sitting at a table in the middle of the speakeasy. Several visitors claim to have sensed them as well.

The Volstead Act passed in 1919 prohibited the production, sale, or purchase of liquor containing more than 0.5 percent alcohol content. As a result, illegal stills sprang up nearly over-night. In Butte, so many people were "stilling" during Prohi-bition that the city's sewer system was overwhelmed by all the mash poured into it. Meanwhile, organized gangs of boot-leggers smuggled liquor across the border from Canada. Much of it was sold in illegal bars or "speakeasies," so-called be-cause customers had to softly "speak easy," when ordering drinks so they wouldn't be overheard by federal agents.

Some of the speakeasies were quite elaborate, hidden be-hind false paneling in legitimate nightclubs. Many had bullet-proof doors, two-way mirrors, and secret exits in case of a raid. While the police were battling their way through the doors, employees would quickly dispose of anything that could be used as evidence.

As one young tour guide discovered in 2004, two spirits from those wild and exhilarating days still linger at the Rookwood Speakeasy.

J.P. "Josh" Johnson is a college student majoring in history and philosophy. In 2004 he joined Old Butte Historical Ad-ventures as a tour guide. At the time, the young company was cleaning and fixing up a number of dilapidated historical buildings. Among them was the recently discovered Rookwood Speakeasy.

"The Rookwood wasn't the only speakeasy in Butte," Johnson said, "but it was one of the most lavish, one of the better places in town. I was in college and I needed money. Giving tours was a great evening job for me. Whenever we had a big event like Irish Days, we'd open up the speakeasy and dress in period clothes.

"The buildings we were renovating were abandoned and most didn't have electric power, so we used flashlights to take people around. It made for a very eerie tour. The speak-easy was always the last stop, the climax of the tour. There were no lights in the stairwell, so I would go down with my flashlight, turn on the power in the speakeasy, and then come back to guide people down the stairs with my flashlight. After the tour, I walked people back up the stairs, went back down to turn off the lights , then locked up and went home.

"I'll never forget what happened one night in late July or early August, right about the time we were working on the old speakeasy. That particular night I felt something strange when I went down the stairs to turn the lights on. It felt like something was out of place, but I blew it off. After the tour, I walked the people back up the stairs as usual and we said our goodbyes. I was sure that all of them had come out with me, because it was my habit to keep track of how many I had on the tour in a little notebook I carried with me. That way, if I lost some of them, I could go back and look for them.

"After they had all left, I went back down and opened the bulletproof door and walked into the speakeasy. All I had to do was shut off the lights and then I could head on home. Suddenly I noticed a couple of gentlemen sitting at a table in the middle of the room. One had a fedora hat and a moustache. The other wore a flat straw hat and was clean-shaven. I think he had a crew-cut. Both of them were dressed in pinstriped suits like they wore in the twenties. They were just sitting there looking at each other. Their hands were around the glasses we had sitting on the table.

"They didn't seem to notice me and they didn't say a word. They were just sitting there with drinks in their hands. The first thing I thought of saying was, 'You gentlemen will have to leave. It's time to lock up!' Then it struck me that these guys hadn't been there when I brought the tour through, and they shouldn't be there now.

"I must have stared at them for two or three minutes. Then the guy with the mustache turned and gave me a casual look like you'd give someone who just walked into a restaurant. I just freaked and took off running. I stood outside for ten minutes, wondering what the hell had just happened. Then I put two and two together and called Dennis Dutton, my boss, and said, 'Dennis, there's somebody down here in the old speakeasy!'"

Johnson's boss confirmed the story. "Josh was practically babbling when he called me," Dutton reported. "He kept saying, 'I'm not crazy, I'm not crazy!' I told him to hang on and I'd be right down. When I got there we went through the speakeasy together. No one else was there. Since then, about half a dozen people on tours have said they sensed something down there, but nobody reported seeing anything."

Later, Johnson was curious enough to try to find out who the ghosts were. He looked through old photos at the Butte Archives, but couldn't match the faces he'd seen to any well-known people of that time. He also checked to see who had owned the building, but that person's description didn't match what he'd seen either.

"Once in a while Dennis will ask me to take some people down there in the winter," Johnson said. "Every time I go down there I open up that door and look both ways because I want to see those guys again. They were as plain as day and they didn't fit in our time period. The guy with the moustache kind of resembled Paul Newman in *The Sting*, but his nose was rounder and flatter. The other man was clean-shaven, with a round face. He was probably in his fifties and had a pocket watch in his vest with a really fancy watch chain. His suit was brown or dark purple. The other guy was about six feet tall. His legs didn't fit under the table very well. I don't recall if they cast shadows, but I do remember that it smelled smoky down there, cigar or cigarette smoke. There was a little Italian restaurant upstairs at the time, but no smoking was allowed there. It must have been about ten P.M. when I saw them. In the old days, the place would have been swinging that time of night."

According to their website, "Old Butte Historical Adventures was established in 2004 by a small group of local historians and property owners working together to preserve and display the colorful history of Butte." The group offers several walking tours as well as longer day trips to nearby ghost towns. Frank, Sue, and I signed up for the city tour, led by Caleb, a young man nattily dressed in a 1920s-era dark-blue pinstriped suit and a fedora. The nearly two-hour walking tour included the historic Hirbour barbershop, the old city jail, and the tour company's star attraction, the recently discovered Rookwood Speakeasy, considered the "most beautiful speakeasy west of Chicago."

Caleb proved a master storyteller and soon had our group of nine fascinated by his tales of the seamier side of Butte's history. The barbershop was our first stop. During Prohibition a speakeasy was concealed behind a wall; the barbers supplemented their income by selling shots of booze. One barber was rarely waiting in the shop, but prospective customers could run him to earth in one of his four favorite bars.

The old City Hall Jail was built in 1890 and closed in 1971 after a prisoner mysteriously died. Upon inspection, conditions in the jail were found to be so inhumane that all prisoners were immediately transferred to another facility. One of its most famous temporary occupants was daredevil Evel Knievel.

We would probably have walked past the Rookwood Hotel without a second glance if we hadn't been with Caleb. The hotel has a surprisingly narrow front and doesn't catch the eye, but according to Caleb that will change when the exterior is repainted.

Caleb unlocked the door and led us down marble steps to the entrance of the speakeasy. In 1920, the lobby had been moved from the basement to the second floor, and the former lobby converted to this speakeasy. Each day a new password was placed in certain advertisements in the daily newspaper; those "in the know" knew where to look for the new password. Despite all the precautions, however, the speakeasy was raided by U.S. Treasury agents at least twice.

The speakeasy may have been used as an illegal saloon until at least 1950, when the building changed hands and became the LaSalle Apartments. Gradually the existence of the speakeasy was forgotten, its door blocked by heaps of debris. It was rediscovered when Mike Byrnes, co-founder of Old Butte Historical Adventures, was given permission by the new owner to explore the derelict building. Byrnes found this historical treasure behind a three-inch-thick wooden door.

There was a collective gasp of delight when we followed Caleb inside. The speakeasy seemed eerily alive. It felt like any moment we would find ourselves in a smoke-filled room crowded with flappers and young men in zoot suits gambling, drinking, and listening to the latest 1920s jazz. The room is beautiful, with terrazzo flooring, stained-glass skylights, and original hardwood. The bar and the back bar are original, as is a 1920s-era radio and a two-way mirror positioned beside the entrance so the bartender could see who was at the door without being observed himself. A number of tables scattered around the room are draped with red tablecloths that give the speakeasy a festive air. On one wall a photo shows the young William Boyd, better known later in his career as Hopalong Cassidy.

When the speakeasy was discovered in 2004, an old Stetson hat sporting a "Hoover for President" pin was found hanging on the wall. Butte was an overwhelmingly Democratic town and anyone supporting a Republican candidate in 1928 would have encountered heated opposition. I wondered if the hat's owner ever left the speakeasy or if he ended up entombed behind the wall, his lone hat a gruesome reminder of his fate.

Although I was aware of Josh Johnson's experience at the speakeasy before we signed up for the tour, I knew nothing about the Hirbour barbershop or the old city jail. When I listened to the tape I had made in those locations, I discovered that ghostly whispers had been caught in both the barbershop and the jail. Butte's colorful past, it seems, never completely fades away.

Old Butte Historical Adventures offers a variety of fascinating tours. It's likely that many of the historical buildings you'll visit are haunted, so why not take a tape recorder or a camera and try your luck at capturing ghostly voices or images from the past?

SENTENCED TO
ETERNITY

OLD MONTANA TERRITORIAL PRISON
1106 Main Street
Deer Lodge, Montana 59722
406-846-3111

Ghostly Activity Level: High

HISTORY: The Montana Territorial Prison was built in Deer Lodge 1869–70, primarily with convict labor. In 1893 the original 12-foot-high wood fence was replaced with the 24-foot-high turreted sandstone wall that still surrounds the prison grounds. The prison was in active use until September 29, 1979, when a new prison was constructed four miles west of town. The old prison, now listed on the National Register of Historic Places, is a museum complex that tourists can explore at their leisure or with guides, many of whom are former prison guards. Living conditions in the early days were primitive for guards and prisoners both, and punishments brutal. Many prisoners tried to escape by tunneling under the wall, but none succeeded. In 1908, an escape attempt left the deputy warden dead and Warden Frank Conley seriously wounded. The two inmates involved were hanged on the grounds. In 1959, a deputy warden was killed and 20 prison guards taken hostage during a riot. The National Guard was called in and fired three bazooka rounds at the Cell House tower to which the ringleaders had retreated. The marks left by the bazookas are visible today.

PHENOMENA: A former guard and the tour group he had led into the Cell House saw a ghostly blue light near Cell Number 1, where convicted murderer Paul "Turkey Pete" Eitner lived until his death in 1967. Several former guards claim to have recognized the ghost of "Turkey Pete" in the burned-out theater where he had often attended boxing matches. Visitors to the maximum security building have noticed intense cold and a foul odor coming from one of the cells used for solitary confinement, and at least one tourist claims to have been pushed back up the stairs by an invisible force. Ghostly voices were recorded in various buildings. Although the theater burned down in 1976, the stench of charred wood is at times strong enough to make visitors' eyes water. Photographs taken of the gallows displayed in the theater have shown white vortices and mists.

My friend Pat Cody and I drove up to Deer Lodge on a hot July day in 2000. The gray sandstone walls and towers of Montana's first state prison loomed above the main street, as solid and impressive now as when they were built in 1893.

We parked across the street and hurried to the visitor center. A group of people milled around, waiting for the guided tour to begin. When we heard that former prison guard Boyd Gutebier would lead the tour, Pat and I quickly bought tickets, for who would be more likely to know whether there was any truth to stories about a haunting at the prison than a former guard?

Gutebier stood to one side, a tall, grim-faced man whose watchful gaze missed nothing around him. As soon as the last ticket had been sold, Gutebier stepped forward and introduced himself in a voice that carried easily to the back of the crowd. His tour, he announced flatly, was "tell it like it was," unlike the cleaned-up accounts of other guides.

We followed him into the sweltering prison yard and over to the concrete slab where the 1896 Cell House had stood. Both convicts and guards suffered hardships in the early days, he told us. The prison was bitterly cold in the winter and baking hot in the summer. Each prisoner had a bucket for water and one for human waste. Prisoners would sometimes hurl the contents of their waste buckets at the guards. Punishment was swift: the convict would be forcibly stripped, shackled between two cells, and doused with buckets of icy water, even during frigid winter weather. It wasn't until 1912, when the next Cell House was built, that prisoners had running water and toilets.

Gutebier then led us over to the shell of the W. A. Clark Theater. The theater had been built by convict labor with materials donated by W. A. Clark, Jr. It opened in 1920. Prisoners who had earned the privilege could attend band concerts, plays, boxing matches, and religious services there.

The prison was gutted by fire in December 1976. Arson was suspected, but no one was ever charged with the crime. According to Gutebier, however, the fire was set to destroy clues to an incident in June 1975, when the prison's band director was brutally beaten by convicts in the theater. He had apparently stepped out for a few minutes, leaving a group of convicts practicing music. When he returned, he may have seen something he shouldn't have, and was jumped and beaten. The convicts were well aware that prison officials would spare no effort to find out what had happened, so they burned down the theater six months later to destroy any evidence they might have left. In the process, a number of convicts from competing gangs were beaten, and several died.

Officially, however, no connection was ever made between the beating of the band director and the destruction of the theater, nor was any mention made of convict deaths.

The doors of the theater stood open. Our fellow tourists crowded inside, perhaps as much to escape the blazing sun as to look at the gallows set up inside. This was the notorious "galloping gallows" used for judicial executions in early-day Montana. When an execution was scheduled, the gallows were disassembled and shipped to the sheriff of that county. At least nine lives were ended on this galloping gallows.

Pat and I waited until most of the tour group had come back outside, and stepped into the shadowy entrance to look at the gallows. A wire barrier stretched across the passage a few yards ahead, but we were still several feet from it when the stench of charred wood struck us almost like a physical blow. Pat's eyes began to water, and I could literally taste the smoke. We retreated hastily. Only later did we begin to wonder how an odor could persist so strongly for over a quarter century in Deer Lodge's harsh climate, and why no one else had commented on it.

Next stop on the tour was the Cell House built in 1912. We stopped in front of Cell Number 1. Gutebier said it was a model facility at the time. Prison life consisted of hard work during the day, solitary confinement at night, and silence at all times. As the number of prisoners grew, it eventually became necessary to place two men in each cell—each cell, that is, except Cell Number 1, the long-time home of Paul "Turkey Pete" Eitner.

Eitner was convicted of murder in 1918 and spent the rest of his life in prison, dying in 1967 at age 89. He was a colorful character put in charge of the prison's turkey flock, and soon earned the sobriquet "Turkey Pete." As the years passed and he gradually lost hope of ever being released, he retreated into a fantasy world. One day he sold the entire turkey flock to a farmer for 25 cents each. After that, he became a prison entrepreneur. Inmates printed checks in the prison print shop, and he used them to "purchase" the prison, writing checks to the guards for their salaries. In his delusions, Eitner also believed he had sold grasshopper legs to Fidel Castro, bought an Alaskan fishing fleet and a stable of racehorses, and sent a check for $10 million to Brazil to help save the coffee crop.

A model prisoner, the aging "Turkey Pete" was allowed by prison authorities to roam freely in and out of his cell. As he grew older, he slept on a couch in the visitor's lounge. When he died, his cell was retired and converted to a barbershop. His funeral took place in the W. A. Clark Theater, the only funeral ever held within the walls of the prison.

Boyd Gutebier paused in his storytelling, and looked directly at Pat and me. I had asked him before the start of the tour about ghosts at the prison, but he hadn't had time to reply. "I don't usually talk about ghosts unless somebody asks," he said somberly, "but I know what I saw."

One day, Gutebier told us, he had been talking to another group of tourists who had been standing right where we presently stood, in front of Cell Number One. Suddenly Gutebier saw a flash of blue light above and just behind his tour group. He never found an explanation for the strange light, and concluded that it was the ghost of "Turkey Pete." Other guards have seen "Pete's" ghost floating in midair in the ruins of the theater. "Pete" had spent many happy hours attending events there, and of course his funeral was held there.

With that, Gutebier headed toward the door, and we all crowded close at his heels. I was relieved to see that Pat and I weren't the only ones glancing in all directions, just in case "Turkey Pete" decided to make a belated appearance!

Our final stop was the old Women's Prison, converted into

Maximum Security cells in 1959. Gutebier described the brutal punishments for any infraction of the rules. "Men are easy to break," Gutebier stated. And indeed, a sense of overwhelming misery still lingers in those cells. Tourists have reported areas of intense cold, a foul odor, and a threatening sense of presence in certain parts of the building. One woman complained of being pushed by an invisible force.

Oddly enough, I sensed nothing unusual in the maximum security cells. Instead, I felt drawn back to the gutted shell of the theater. This time, the entrance was empty and we were able to approach the wire barrier without having to squeeze past other tourists. Something seemed different, though. The stench of charred wood was completely gone! Pat and I exchanged quizzical glances. How could an odor strong enough to cause our eyes to water have dissipated so quickly?

Odors are one of the most common types of paranormal phenomena, ranging from the pleasant to the unspeakably foul. Not everyone in a group will be able to detect the smell, but to those who can, it will be very real. Perhaps what we experienced was a psychic scent, a "leftover" from the past.

We pressed against the wire barrier that blocked the entrance, thrust our cameras through, and started snapping photos. I finished up a pack of Polaroid film and switched to my 35mm camera. As the Polaroids began to develop, I noticed something odd: white vortexes were beginning to develop. I said hastily to Pat, "Quick, take more photos—there's something!"

The two Polaroid photos show several white vortexes swirling around the gallows, and then moving off to the right. One of my 35mm shots shows the vortices beginning to fade away. Pat's photos, on the other hand, showed a perfectly normal scene: the gallows and the interior of the theater. We were elated. Not only had we experienced what was almost certainly a psychic odor in the theater, but the photos supported the evidence of our own senses.

The prison wasn't done with us yet, however. The next day I was on the phone with a friend, describing what had happened, when my living room was filled with the incredibly strong, acrid odor of charred wood. I do have a wood-burning stove but it had not been used for several months. The odor lingered for a few minutes, and then went away.

Why not try your own luck at the prison? Be sure to take photos, and keep a tape recorder running—if you can! Ghostly voices have been recorded in various areas of the prison. Not all the convicts, it seems, moved to the new prison in 1978.

Postscript: In August 2005 I returned to the prison with my friends Frank and Sue. While in the main cell block, I paused in front of "Turkey Pete's" cell, describing what I saw. I inexplicably stumbled over Eitler's name twice, mispronouncing it as "Eisler," and when I played the tape back, a whispery male voice gently corrects me: "*Eit*-ler." Later, in The Hole, a dark cell where convicts were kept in solitary confinement, I commented into my tape recorder, "Tourists sometimes report icy cold, a foul stench, and a sense of evil in this cell." The same ghostly voice on my tape adds, "Yep!"

Ghosts and artifacts from the past aren't the only attractions worth your attention at the Montana Territorial Prison. Just across the street are Yesterday's Playthings, Montana's foremost doll and toy museum; the Frontier Museum with its large collection of cowboy collectibles; the Powell County Museum featuring military weapons and a jukebox collection; and the Gun Port Theatre, where musicals and comedies are performed on summer evenings.

THE GRANT-KOHRS
RANCH

GRANT-KOHRS RANCH
National Historic Site
Deer Lodge, Montana 59722
406-846-2070 x. 224

Ghostly Activity Level: Moderate

HISTORY: Canadian fur trader Johnny Grant built the main house in 1862 and used it as a trading post and headquarters for his ranching operations. He married several times, taking wives from local Indian tribes to establish friendly relations with them. The discovery of gold brought an influx of miners, camp followers, and outlaws to the area, and Grant became concerned for his family's safety. In 1866 Grant sold his house and moved back to Canada with his family.

The new owner was Conrad Kohrs, who had led an adventurous life as sailor, merchant, miner, and butcher. At one time Kohrs had as many as 50,000 cattle on ten million acres of open range, earning him the title "Cattle King of Montana." In 1868, Kohrs married Augusta Kruse. In 1890, they added several rooms to the house, nearly doubling its size, and furnished it in the latest style.

In 1901, their 21-year-old son William died unexpectedly. For years afterward, the grieving Augusta kept his bedroom as it had been when he had occupied it. In 1920, Conrad Kohrs died. Augusta moved to Helena, returning to the ranch each summer until her own death in 1945. Grandson Conrad Kohrs Warren managed the ranch after his grandfather's death and bought it from his grandmother in 1940. In 1972, the ranch was designated a National Historic Site and today is administered by the National Park Service as a rare intact example of a nineteenth-century working ranch.

PHENOMENA: The scent of lavender, favored by Augusta Kohrs, is noticed occasionally in the house. Objects are sometimes moved from their usual places. The voices of two cowboys were heard in one of the barns, along with the sound of grain being poured into a bucket. Visitors sometimes remark on an air of great sadness in the house. A gruff male voice was picked up on audiotape during a tour, though only the tour guide was speaking at the time.

The Grant-Kohrs Ranch was the home of the pioneering Kohrs family from 1866 to the early 1970s. The ranch today consists of 1,500 acres and over 90 historical structures set in a broad valley with a spectacular view of the Pintler Range in the distance. The main house is set among trees several hundred yards from the parking lot, reached via a long path that dips beneath the railroad tracks.

The morning was already uncomfortably warm when we arrived, so we stopped in the shade of the railway trestle to take photos of longhorn cattle in a nearby pasture before continuing to the house. The previous tour had just ended and the next one wouldn't begin for a few more minutes, so Frank, Sue, and I split up to explore the nearby buildings. I knew that there had been some apparently paranormal activity in one of the barns, so I headed for the first one I saw, a low red barn down behind the house. This barn had a wide aisle with stalls along each side, lighted by huge incandescent bulbs hung above each stall. The stalls were filled with antique farm wagons and obviously had not been used by horses for quite a while.

I felt an odd stillness the moment I entered the barn. I can only describe it as a sense of stagnant time, and I've often encountered it in haunted sites. I hesitated, looking around. No one else was there, although I could hear a group of people approaching from outside. I started to walk toward the back of the barn, hoping to examine the wagons before anyone else came in. Just then the right-hand lightbulb closest to the back wall blinked slowly off and then on again. For a moment I thought someone had used a dimmer switch, but no one was visible. Even if the light had overheated and an overload switch had shut the bulb off, it would have happened instantly, not gradually. I stood watching all the lights for a few seconds but nothing else happened.

Trudging back up the hill toward the house, I met a National Park Service ranger and stopped to talk to her. In my experience, most Park Service employees are reluctant to talk about ghosts, but this young woman readily agreed to tell me about some of the odd experiences she and others had had at the ranch, provided I did not use her name.

"Ranger X" had been posted at the Grant-Kohrs Ranch for about 18 months. She had formerly been stationed at Independence Hall in Philadelphia, Pennsylvania, and at the Lincoln House in Springfield, Illinois, both known to be haunted. She was open-minded about the possibility of ghosts.

I told her about the odd behavior of the lightbulb. She hadn't heard of any paranormal activity in that barn, but acknowledged that a colleague had experienced something very odd in another barn not far from the house.

By now Frank and Sue had rejoined me, and Ranger X led

us over to another barn, also red but much taller than the first. It had been built in the 1870s to house the draft horses. Inside we were greeted by the familiar scent of horses and hay. The horses were out in the paddock for the day, but their harnesses were hung neatly on hooks beside the stalls. Everything seemed quite ordinary. According to Ranger X, however, this was where Chief Ranger Matt Connor had experienced something very odd back in 2001.

It was a stormy October afternoon, and Connor was in a hurry to lock up and go home. He set the alarm in the main house and began to secure the outbuildings. He noticed that the big red barn's door stood open, although he was certain it had been padlocked earlier. He shut the door and was about to padlock it when he heard boots crossing the floor inside. There seemed to be two men, talking quietly to each other. Then Connor heard the lid of the grain bin open, and the rattle of grain being poured into a bucket. He opened the door and peered inside. The sounds cut off instantly and no one was visible. As soon as he shut the door, however, the sounds resumed.

It was beginning to get dark and Connor was anxious to get home, so he locked the door and left the invisible cowboys to their work.

Odd things happen in the main house, too, according to Ranger X. "There's a piano in the parlor," she told me. "We only play it at Christmas or at the Western Heritage event in July. Every now and then, though, one of our rangers will wash her hands and play it. One day a ranger was playing it, but she wasn't playing classical music, and her hands got ice cold. She didn't think much of it, but another time she went back again and she wasn't playing classical music and her hands turned icy cold again. But yet, if you play classical music, it's not a problem."

I knew Augusta Kohrs loved music and traveled to New York City each year to attend the opera. Perhaps this was her way of gently protesting the ranger's choice of music.

"One time," Ranger X continued, "one of the rangers was having a really bad day, and she was just coming down from checking the third floor when she was overwhelmed by the aroma of lavender. It was very calming. Augusta Kohrs used a lavender scent. And then there's the floor scrubber in the kitchen—it's historic, so we lay it down on the floor because we don't want the bristles to get ruined. Every now and then we walk in the house and it's standing up. We'll put it down again, and come back to find it standing up again. Sometimes towels in the bathroom are moved and no one will admit to touching them. In John Bielenberg's room, (Conrad Kohr's half-brother and partner) his hat will be moved somewhere else."

It was time for our house tour, so I thanked the ranger and we joined the crowd gathered around the guide, Barb Young. She is a retired nurse from Texas who volunteers at different historic house museums each summer. After the tour, I asked whether she had had any ghostly experiences at this house.

"I haven't myself," she replied, "although I've had some odd experiences during my career as an oncology nurse. I did have a group of young people from Japan here, and they had a translator from Butte. They were high school students. After we had done the whole tour they were waiting for the next group to come around, and this young man from the first group came up and said something to the translator, and she asked, 'Has anything bad happened in this house? It seems tragic.'

"I said, 'Well, nothing tragic in the house, but there has been some real sadness in the house. Johnny Grant's third wife, Cora, the one he probably loved the most, died shortly after he sold the house. He was in Canada, and she died somewhere around here, though not in the house, after bearing her sixth child. Then William Kohrs died while he was away at college. Augusta would dust his room every day, keeping it just as it was when he was alive.' Nothing I had said during the tour would have given the student a clue, especially since it all had to go through a translator."

According to paranormal researchers, strong emotion can imprint on the surroundings and occasionally be detected by sensitive people. Perhaps Augusta Kohrs' grief over her son's untimely death left such an imprint. On the other hand, it's possible that Augusta herself may still revisit the house she loved so much. It would have been very much in character for this kind-hearted woman to offer comfort to a distraught ranger.

Augusta Kohrs may not be the only spirit to visit the house. When I replayed the tape I had made of the tour, I heard an unfamiliar voice just as Barb Young was telling us about Conrad Kohrs Warren's decision in the 1950s to allow a ranch manager to use the upstairs bedroom and the 1890s bathroom. At that point, a gruff male voice chipped in with "Yeah."

And what was it that Chief Ranger Connor heard coming from the red barn that stormy October day? The sounds have not been heard again, so perhaps the footsteps and the voices were a sort of recording from the past rather than actual spirits. One thing's sure, though—no one lingers near the red barn at closing time.

The Grant-Kohrs Ranch provides a fascinating look at late nineteenth-century ranch life. You'll be able to step inside an original bunkhouse and see how the cowboys actually lived, and even watch a blacksmith at work. Don't forget to look inside the big red barn. Perhaps you'll be the next one to hear the ghostly cowboys going about their chores as they did so long ago.

RESCUED BY
A GHOST

FORT PECK SUMMER THEATRE
Fort Peck, Montana 59223
406-526-9943

Ghostly Activity Level: Moderate

HISTORY: The area around Fort Peck was first settled in the 1860s, when a trading post was built on a ledge overlooking the Missouri River. In 1933, during the depths of the Depression, President Franklin Delano Roosevelt authorized construction of a huge earth-filled dam to create jobs for thousands of workers. The dam was designed to produce hydroelectric power as well as control floodwaters and improve navigation downstream. Between 1934 and the dam's completion in 1940, over 40,000 people came to Fort Peck. Dormitory housing was quickly filled and shantytowns sprang up nearby to house most of the workers, many of whom were accompanied by their families. On September 22, 1938, a section of the newly completed dam shifted. Men and machinery were swept into the Missouri along with five million cubic yards of earth. Eight men died. The bodies of six were never recovered. Many of the buildings used by construction workers still exist and are listed in the National Register of Historic Buildings.

PHENOMENA: Since the early 1970s, unexplained activity has been reported by those who work in the theatre. Live theatrical productions are offered during the summer and a number of people have had ghostly encounters in the old building. Footsteps and voices are often heard in the lobby when no one is visible, lights turn themselves on, and a ghost described as a man wearing workman's clothes of the 1930s has been seen in the balcony.

The Fort Peck Theatre, like the historic Fort Peck Hotel, was built in a style called Depression Swiss Chalet. Opened in 1934, the theatre's massive auditorium held over 1,200 people. There was little to entertain the workers and their families, so first-run movies were offered around the clock for the six years the dam was under construction. In winter, people crowded into the theatre, one of the few heated buildings in town, as much to keep warm as to see a show.

The theatre operated as a movie house until 1968, when demolition became a real possibility. The Fort Peck Fine Arts Council was formed in 1970 to preserve the building, and in 1971 the first summer season of theatrical productions was begun.

Over the years, many types of paranormal phenomena have been reported. The ghost of a man dressed in workman's clothes has been seen in the balcony. He is considered a helpful ghost, and is affectionately called "Floyd," after Floyd Sunderhauf, the first manager of the theatre.

The evening we arrived was warm and beautiful, so Frank, Sue, and I strolled over to the theatre from the Fort Peck Hotel. The theatre's marquee was brightly lit and its doors open; a line of people stood at the box office window. Once inside, we bought a program from one of the volunteers and walked to the auditorium. Over 1,200 people could be seated in the cavernous space, but nowadays the audience is much smaller, averaging about 200 for each performance.

The stage was set for the performance of *Picasso at the Lapin Agile*. As the audience settled into their seats, there was an almost palpable sense of anticipation and excitement in the air.

We had chosen to sit about halfway back on the main floor, in front of a barrier that separated us from the mass of seats just below us. No one else was seated nearby. Just as the lights dimmed, I thought I glimpsed two or three shadowy children running past me. Each grabbed the curved top of the barrier in front of us and quickly rolled over it to drop to the floor about four feet below. It seemed to be a game, repeated several times. It was my imagination almost certainly, for the sense of history was so strong in that building we could almost feel the jostling of the thousands of men, women, and children who had crowded in here.

The performance was enjoyable, with plenty of clever one-liners, and the cast received a well-deserved ovation. We lingered while the audience filed out, for I had previously asked to be introduced after the performance to any of the cast who had encountered the ghost. As it turned out, only one member of the current cast had experienced anything odd in the theatre. He was Christopher Kristant, who played Picasso in this show. Kristant lived in California most of the year but had spent the last several summers at the Fort Peck Theatre.

"I've always been somewhat of a believer," he acknowledged. When he stayed at the haunted Fort Peck Hotel in 2002, he had quickly realized that the hotel was haunted, but he hadn't heard any ghost stories about the theatre until about a third of the way through that summer.

The ghost, Kristant told us, was named for the first manager of the theatre, Floyd Sunderhauf, who came from Scobey, Montana. Legend has it that he perished in the building after he fell from a long ladder while changing the ceiling lightbulbs. Since records show that Sunderhauf died in Bremerton, Washington, in 1967, that version of the legend is clearly inaccurate. It's certainly possible that someone else may have been killed in an accident at the site, however, and it does seem as if the ghost, whoever he may have been, does keep a watchful eye on anyone who attempts to change the lightbulbs.

"We work here late at night quite often," Kristant said. "You can see how high the beams are. To get up to the lights you need a forty-foot extension ladder. Our lighting designer happened to be up there one night working by himself. He had one hand on the beam and was working on a light. He shifted too far and the extension ladder started to slide along the beam. It got right to the edge of the beam and he felt it stop. Then it righted itself. It would have been impossible for the lighting designer to do that himself. At that point he was so shaken that he got down off the ladder, packed everything up, and left."

According to earlier reports, the lighting designer wasn't the only one to have been rescued from a disastrous fall by an unseen force. Since the 1970s, several actors have claimed that *something* kept them from toppling off ladders or plunging down stairways.

But the ghost's repertoire includes much more than preventing a nasty accident. Cold spots that move, the sounds of men working in a darkened, empty building, and mysterious footsteps in various parts of the theatre have been encountered by dozens of people over the years.

The dressing rooms are not immune from ghostly activity. "Another summer," Kristant recalled, "the gentleman I shared the dressing room with thought he saw someone in our dressing room. He had gone to the room to do something and happened to glance in the mirror. Someone was standing behind him. When he turned around to see who it was, there wasn't anyone there."

"Could he describe what he saw?" I asked.

Kristant shook his head. "He just saw a shape, a figure behind him reflected in the mirror."

He pointed toward a balcony door high above us. "Many times when I'm on stage I'll look out and see the balcony door located stage-left open, and see something coming through the door. And we've all seen lights come on in the auditorium at times, and sometimes in the old projector room. Late at night people working on stage will hear what sounds like a group of people having a party in the lobby. They'll go out there to check and there's nothing going on."

Kristant's gaze lingered on the balcony, where the ghost of the man in tan workman's clothing from the 1930s has been seen. "There definitely is a very strong presence in this building. I'm not normally bothered by it, but sometimes when I'm sitting in my office, I'll just know there's something going on in the building."

Be sure to take in a performance at the Fort Peck Summer Theatre. You'll be impressed by the quality of the performances as well as by the building itself. And if you linger for a few minutes after the audience has left, look around carefully. "Floyd" may just decide to make a dramatic show of his own.

FOOTSTEPS ON
THE STAIRS

FORT PECK HOTEL
175 South Missouri Street
Fort Peck, Montana 59223
406-526-3266

Ghostly Activity Level: Moderate

HISTORY: The Fort Peck Hotel was built in sections by the U. S. Army Corps of Engineers and shipped from Omaha, Nebraska to Fort Peck in 1933, where it was reassembled and opened as the Employees' Hotel. The hotel was used to house construction supervisors, architects, engineers, and surveyors hired for the massive dam project that was about to get underway. The architecture has been described as Depression Swiss Chalet. After the dam was completed, two of the hotel's wings were dismantled and taken away to be re-used elsewhere. The historic hotel was updated in 1993 and continues to welcome guests who come to see the dam, watch wildlife, or go hunting, fishing, or boating. It was placed in the National Register of Historic Places in 1986.

PHENOMENA: For many years the cries of a little girl were heard coming from a corridor just off the main lobby. Neighbors saw lights in an unused room on the third floor, and one of two chairs in that room is consistently found turned to the window overlooking the powerhouses. Many people have heard footsteps on the disused third floor.

The Fort Peck Dam project was a monumental New Deal undertaking that transformed an old trading post established in the 1860s to a sprawling expanse of shantytowns that from 1934 to 1940 were home to nearly 40,000 men, women, and children from all over the United States. An article in the *Glasgow Courier* of December 26, 1935 enthused about how quickly a spirit of community had developed among people of such diverse backgrounds, with schools, a library, basket-ball teams, a hospital, and many other services one would expect to find only in a town that had existed for a much longer period of time.

Surely, I thought, such a massive communal effort must have left its mark, and not only on the landscape.

Apparently it has. According to its staff, the Fort Peck Hotel is definitely haunted. I drove up to Fort Peck on a warm afternoon in late August with friends Frank and Sue. I'd seen photos of the hotel, but the reality was overwhelming. The hotel is a sturdy, three-story wood building, its front porch furnished with comfortable rocking chairs where guests can relax and, for a little while at least, enjoy a slow-paced way of life.

Stepping inside the spacious lobby is like stepping back to the 1930s. The floors and walls are of wood, with the pol-ished patina of age. The 70 rooms on the first and second floors are plain but comfortable, carefully renovated in 1993 to bring them up to date but still retain the atmosphere of the 1930s. All but a few rooms now have their own bathrooms, some with claw-foot tubs.

On chilly nights a cheerful fire warms the lobby, where musical gatherings are sometimes held for the enjoyment of guests and locals. A cozy bar near the reception desk does a lively business.

I introduced myself to Sylvia Little, the hotel's busy hostess, who agreed to relate her ghostly experiences later that evening when things quieted down. We ate dinner in the excellent restaurant and then walked over to the haunted Fort Peck Theatre, where I had arranged to interview members of the cast after the performance. We returned about ten o'clock and found Little sitting at the bar, talking with the hotel's manager, John Johnson. The other guests had retired for the night, and Little and Johnson were glad to relax after an unusually busy day.

Little had heard about the hotel's ghost before she took the job in April, but she hadn't expected anything to happen on her very first night in the hotel. "There was a severe electrical storm that night," she began, "and the power went out. I was in my room with my dog. We were the only ones in the hotel. There was a gap between the bottom of the door and the floor, and my dog kept staring at the gap as if she could see someone standing just outside the door. Then I heard screen doors start to slam in the rising wind. I opened my door to go out, but when I called to my dog, she just planted her feet and wouldn't leave the room."

No one was visible in the dark corridor, but still the dog would not leave the room. Little took a flashlight and walked to the lobby, where she added logs to the fire for warmth and to throw welcome light into dark corners. Then she walked around the building, bracing chairs against screen doors to stop them from banging. When she had finished, she could still hear one screen door banging upstairs. She thought the sound came from somewhere up on the disused third floor, and decided it wouldn't be safe to go up there with just a flashlight. Instead, she spoke aloud to the ghost that reportedly haunted the hotel. "I know you're here," she reported saying. "You're supposed to be a friendly ghost. If you're really here, show me." Then she went back to her room.

What happened next was startling. "I was lying on my bed reading, just about to go to sleep, when suddenly a big picture on the wall dropped onto the desk beneath. It could have knocked over the flower vase on the desk, but somehow it didn't. I thought the screws had pulled out of the drywall or the wire had untwisted, so I got up and checked. The screws were still in the drywall and the wire was intact. I said again to the ghost, 'I know you're here, I know you're friendly. Now you get out of my bedroom and go back upstairs and make whatever is banging around up there quit.' Then I hung the picture back up and went to sleep. I slept comfortably for the rest of the night. The next day I went up to the third floor to look for the screen door I was sure had been banging. It had been taken off its hinges and was leaning against the wall."

That's not the only odd thing Little has encountered in the hotel. "Every now and then I've been in the kitchen, over by the stove, and there's something that makes you want to turn and look. It's like someone's there looking at you."

John Johnson has managed the hotel for six years and had a few encounters of his own to tell us about. "Sometimes lights come on by themselves, even when there's no power, and doors slam in unoccupied rooms. We call the ghost 'Ludd,' after one of the early proprietors, although nobody knows for sure who the ghost is. As far I as know, nobody died tragically at the hotel, although there were lots of deaths in the powerhouses while they were building them. Back then they lost so many guys that they didn't even make a report. One story is that a guy fell off the spillway, and they didn't even bother to get him out. They just poured concrete over him and kept going. The cemetery is full of gravestones that say, 'Killed at Fort Peck Dam.'"

Johnson and his brother-in-law used to sit at the bar after hours, talking. "We often heard a little girl crying somewhere in that wing," Johnson said, gesturing across the lobby toward a brightly lit corridor. "My brother-in-law and I would sit here at the bar and listen to her. We walked down that corridor many times, looking for her, but we could never find her. My brother-in-law always felt sorry for her. We lost him a year ago."

He paused, and then said thoughtfully, "Come to think of it, this is the first season I've been here that we haven't heard her. Maybe my brother-in-law took the little girl with him when he crossed over. He was really good with kids, loved kids."

Then he added, "I don't know if I should tell this in front of Sylvia, because it happened in the room Sylvia's got now. One night years ago I was sleeping in that room, and all of a sudden the room got really cold. It felt like someone sat on the edge of the bed. I just lay there on my side. It felt like someone was leaning over me. I didn't open my eyes because I didn't want to see them."

At least one guest has experienced something odd at the hotel. Christopher Kristant, an actor we had interviewed earlier that evening, had stayed at the hotel during the summer of 2002, his first summer working at the theater. In early spring the hotel was not yet open for the season and there were workers in the hotel during the day, but at night Kristant was alone—or so he supposed.

"I would hear footsteps from the third floor," he told me during the interview. "It was very eerie. I sometimes went up to the second floor and walked along the corridor, listening for footsteps above me. Since there were no guests on the second floor, all the room doors were standing open. Sometimes as I passed the open rooms I would catch glimpses of 'things' from the corner of my eye. Not just beds and dressers. I couldn't really see them clearly enough to define what they were. And sometimes I would hear voices, but I couldn't make out what they were saying."

By now it was close to eleven o'clock and the hotel was quiet. Manager John Johnson had to be back on duty at five in the morning, so he left for home after suggesting that we might like to go in search of ghosts. Sue, Sylvia, and I were eager to do so, but Frank decided to remain at the bar to finish reading his book, rather than tackle three flights of stairs. Little led Sue and me up the stairs to the second floor, where she unlocked the door of the stairway that led to the haunted third floor.

The third floor is presently unused. The rooms are about ten feet by ten feet and have just enough room for a single bed and a dresser. A foot-long piece of wire stretched between two nails would have held a few clothes hangers.

"These rooms were called 'hot cots,'" Little told us. "They ran three shifts around the clock while the dam was being built, and three men would take turns in each bed. As soon as one man came off shift, the man in the bed would have to get up and the next would take his place. The bed never had a chance to cool off."

We peered inside each room as we moved from one end of the hallway to the other. Some were empty, but most contained pieces of old furniture. Little beckoned us into one small room that had a window overlooking the massive powerhouses in the distances. Two red chairs were beside the window, one turned around as though someone had been sitting there enjoying the view.

"This is the chair that is always found facing the window,"

she said. "No matter how many times we put it back, when we go upstairs it'll be turned around again. The neighbors say sometimes they can see lights in here at night, and when we check no one's up here."

I looked out the window at the powerhouses. Men had died building them, I knew; almost every issue of the *Glasgow Courier* for 1935 carried the names of those who had been severely injured or killed while working on the project. Some were crushed by slate falling from the roofs of tunnels or mangled by heavy equipment, while others drowned, suffered broken bones, or died from pneumonia contracted in the bitter winters. The list seemed endless. Yet there had been a sense of community here, as the newspaper had noted. Despite the suffering and the privation, there had been a sense of pride, of hope, of accomplishment. Why should it be surprising if perhaps one of those who had taken part in the largest public works project at the time should have stayed behind, perhaps to sit in that red chair overlooking the powerhouses, nostalgically recalling times long past?

Almost reluctantly, I followed the others out of that room. We hadn't quite reached the centrally located stairway to the lower floors when we all heard three footsteps coming up the stairs. We exchanged questioning glances. The door at the bottom had been firmly closed, and it squeaked loudly whenever it was opened. None of us had heard the door open.

Sylvia Little hung over the railing, looking down the stairs. "Who's there?" she called. No one answered. We waited about 30 seconds, and then heard two more footsteps on the stairs. This time all three of us looked over the railing. The wooden stairs gleamed empty in the light, and the door at the bottom was still closed tight.

We went down to the second floor, waited while Little locked the door behind us, then continued to the first floor lobby without encountering anyone. When we entered the bar where Frank was waiting, he looked up from his book and asked, "Did you just come down now?"

"Yes," I replied. "Why?"

"Oh," he said nonchalantly, "about two chapters ago I heard someone come down the steps and I looked over, expecting to see the three of you. There was nobody on the stairs."

No one he could see, at any rate.

Apparently the ghost, whoever he was, decided to roam the first-floor corridors that night. Sue's room was just down the hall from the room where both Little and Johnson had encountered the ghost. When Sue awoke the next morning the chair in her room showed an impression as though someone had been sitting there. It had not been noticeable when she went to bed. She took a photo of it just in case, and a large orb showed up on the photo, perched just above the chair.

The next morning Sue and I decided to explore the second floor of the hotel. The guests who had stayed there the night before had already checked out, for the room doors were standing wide open, ready for the maids to clean. I opened the screen door to the balcony at one end of the corridor and took a few photos of the powerhouses. After making sure the screen door was securely closed, Sue and I walked down the hallway to the other balcony and took several more photos. Again I was careful to close the screen door behind me. No one else was on either balcony or on the stairs leading down. We then walked back to the central staircase, where I paused to take another photo of the beautiful wood paneling. At that moment we both heard the unmistakable slam of a screen door from one of the balconies.

We glanced quickly from one end of the corridor to the other. No one was in sight in the hallway or on either balcony.

To the best of our knowledge we were the only persons on that floor at that time. Had someone unseen joined us as we took photos from one of the balconies? It wouldn't surprise me in the least. Those who worked on the dam must have taken great pride in their achievement. Every year a few people return to Fort Peck to show their grandchildren what they accomplished in their younger days. Perhaps some who are no longer living also return, to once more walk the hallways of the Fort Peck Hotel.

The Fort Peck area offers a wide variety of activities, from birdwatching to hunting, fishing, and boating, as well as tours of the dam and other surviving buildings from the 1930s New Deal project. You can stay at the historic Fort Peck Hotel, enjoy dinner at its excellent restaurant, and take in an evening performance at the Fort Peck Summer Theatre. When you return to the hotel from the theater, why not try an experiment? Walk quietly up the stairs and along the second-floor corridor, pausing every now and then to listen. If you hear footsteps above you on the third floor, spare a kind thought for the soul who returns now and then to sit in that red chair by the window, perhaps reminiscing about his part in a project that transformed much of eastern Montana's landscape.

THE LITTLE COWBOY BAR

LITTLE COWBOY BAR
105 West River Street
Fromberg, Montana 59029
406-668-9508

Ghostly Activity Level: Moderate

HISTORY: The building that currently houses the Little Cowboy Bar dates back at least to the 1920s. Over the years it has served as a feed store, a lumberyard, a law office, and as headquarters for the local telephone company. In the early 1950s it became a bar, owned and run by retired farmer Henry Deines. After Deines died in 1971, Shirley Smith bought the bar. Smith, a personal friend of many of the great rodeo performers of earlier days, has added a museum of Western memorabilia at the back of the building. Under her energetic ownership the Little Cowboy Bar continues to be a popular watering hole for locals.

PHENOMENA: According to Lucille Frank and Marjorie Flynn, daughters of former owner Henry Deines, there was no haunting before their father's death in 1971. Since then, however, the figure of a man whose description matches that of Deines has been glimpsed inside the building by people driving past long after the bar has closed for the night. In addition, customers and employees have seen Deines seated at the end of the bar, and a non-functioning radio once blared out a lively accordion tune that Deines, an accomplished accordion player, had composed himself. Deines may not be the only ghost in this historic bar. Areas of intense cold have been noticed in the museum room, and whispered comments by different voices were recorded on audiotape.

On a misty day in October I drove to Fromberg with my friends Frank and Sue to visit the Little Cowboy Bar. Ghost aficionado Dan Damjanovich had tipped me off to the rumor that there was a particularly interesting haunting at the bar. A phone call to Shirley Smith, long-time owner of the bar, confirmed the touching tale of previous owner Henry Deines, who haunted the bar where he died until he was reunited with his beloved wife many years later.

From the outside, the Little Cowboy Bar looked familiar, even though none of us had ever seen it before. The rustic wood building reminded me of the saloons in the old Western movies I had doted on as a kid. It lacked only swinging doors and horses tied to a hitching rack.

Shirley Smith agreed. "The Little Cowboy Bar is a local watering hole," she says, "not one of your fancy yuppie places. It is a throwback to 'those thrilling days of yesteryear.'" The walls are covered with pictures of cowboys, rodeo riders, Indians, and a few famous folks. The museum is a catch-all of cowboy and Indian artifacts, memorabilia, stories of outlaws, and even a bug collection. Amateur historian Shirley and her friend Tom can steer visitors to outdoor sites where ancient Indian rock art can be viewed.

The building is low and narrow, and looks deceptively small from the outside. Once inside, though, we quickly realized that the bar is spacious. The building consists of three rooms arranged shotgun-style. The bar, seating, jukebox, and keno machine occupy the front of the building. In the middle is a smaller room where Henry Deines and his wife once slept. A Coke machine now stands on the spot where Henry died. Shirley's museum is housed in a large room at the rear of the building. The room was added long after Deines' death. It is filled with all sorts of memorabilia that may have come with ghosts of their own.

Shirley was waiting for us, along with Deines' two daughters, Lucille Frank and Marjorie Flynn, as well as several other people who had come to share their ghost stories with us. I quickly introduced my ghost-hunting friends and asked Shirley to tell us about her experiences with the ghost of Henry Deines.

"One day I was fixing a radio," she began. "Everything was out of it, bulbs and all. All of a sudden it just started blaring. Three fellows came in, and we were sitting there talking. It was playing accordion polka music. Henry played an accordion. One of the guys walked over to look at it, and he said, 'It ain't got anything in it!'"

"Then my friend Darlene was tending bar one day," Shirley continued. "She was all alone, and a plate glass mirror just shattered. It scared the wadding out of her. Then other things started happening. The jukebox and the bowling machine would turn themselves on sometimes. Henry was mischievous. Sometimes he would turn the jukebox up just for fun. Once a little girl was playing funky music. We heard loud bangs and ran all over looking for whatever was causing them. We didn't find anything. I yelled, 'All right, Henry, I won't play that music!' And the banging stopped.

"A lady came down from Billings once. She was playing the keno machine over by the bathroom. After a while she came over to complain that a man was staring at her. 'What man?' I asked her. She turned around to point to the end of the bar, then said, 'Where did that man go?' I got a photo of Henry and asked her if that was the man. She said it was."

Henry's daughter Lucille spoke up. "We brought a white teacup poodle here about five years ago. He wouldn't go past the door to the bedroom. He stopped and he started barking." Henry Deines had died in that bedroom, now a passage between the bar and the museum.

Lucille had brought a tape recorder, and played some of Henry's favorite recordings for us. I'm a polka lover, but these were tunes I had never heard before. One of them, lively and expertly played, caused Shirley to exclaim, "That's the song the radio played that time!" The unnamed polka was one of Henry's original compositions.

Not long ago, Shirley picked up a 12-pack of beer to carry to the basement and took a bad fall on the stairs. "Next thing I knew I was sitting on the bottom step," she says. "At the time of the fall I felt absolutely nothing. I should have been badly hurt."

"Do you think Henry might have caught you?" I asked.

"Something did," she answered with absolute certainty. "Something did." As it turned out, she had injured one leg, but her injuries should have been much worse.

Henry's ghost hasn't been seen or sensed since his beloved wife Mary died. The two were very close, and apparently Henry decided to stay around until she could join him. "I felt almost deserted when he went away," Shirley said.

But Henry may not be the only ghost—or former ghost—at the Little Cowboy Bar. Sue, Lucille, Marjorie, and I followed Shirley into the museum. It is large, well lit, and filled with an assortment of amazing objects. Many museums are haunted, presumably by the spirits of former owners anxious to stay near items they treasured in life. Just in case, I made certain that both my tape recorders were running as we entered.

We paused for a few moments before the mannequin of a cowboy, while Shirley told us about some of the great rodeo performers she has known. All of us felt an unusual chill in the area, although the room as a whole was comfortably warm. When I played back the tape later, one of them had picked up a tuneless whistling that sounded while we looked at the mannequin. It was just a few random notes, but none of us had whistled.

On the other side of the room, Shirley pointed out a check written by rodeo rider Bud Linderman the day he was killed in a plane crash, and a newspaper article about the event. "I'll let you read it," she said. At that point, the tape recorder had picked up a whispery male voice murmuring, "It's very good..." and several more words too faint to make out.

My digital camera also captured something unusual: a misty area near the violin form used by rancher–violinmaker Bill Newsome. I didn't mention it to Shirley. A few days later, Shirley phoned to tell me that after we left, she saw mist near the mannequin in the museum, and wondered if someone had been smoking. She doesn't allow smoking in the old building, and the mist faded away when she approached it. The spirits of former owners Henry and Mary Deines may have moved on, but it seems certain that the Little Cowboy Bar has unseen patrons.

Visitors will enjoy the friendly old-time atmosphere of the Little Cowboy Bar, and the museum at the back of the building has a great collection of artifacts. Ghostly voices were recorded in the museum, and a number of people have noticed inexplicable cold spots.

RETURN OF A
MURDER VICTIM?

GALLATIN GATEWAY INN
76405 Gallatin Road
Gallatin Gateway, Montana 59730
406-763-4672

Ghostly Activity Level: Moderate

HISTORY: The Gallatin Gateway Inn was built in 1927 by
the Chicago, Milwaukee, Saint Paul & Pacific Railroad. It
provided summer accommodations for tourists traveling by
train to visit Yellowstone National Park. An early brochure
described the architecture as "semi-Spanish," with tiled roofs,
a veranda, and a huge lounge with fireplace. Tourists would
descend from the train, freshen up at the inn, and board a
fleet of buses for Yellowstone Park, 80 miles away. The Depression of the 1930s had little effect on the Inn's guest list,
but it was forced to close during World War II when millions
of men were shipped overseas and the nation's attention
turned to the war effort. The decline in rail traffic eventually
forced the inn's sale in 1961. It was bought by its present
owners, renovated, and reopened in 1986. It is now open year-
round and attracts anglers, skiers, hikers, and, as always, visitors bound for Yellowstone National Park.

PHENOMENA: According to legend, a young female employee was found dead, probably murdered, in Room 207 sometime in the late 1920s or early 1930s. She may be responsible for the scent of floral perfume sometimes noticed by guests. In 1990, one of the inn's maids saw the ghost of a gentleman in a tuxedo standing on the landing of the staircase that leads into the huge lounge. In 1998, I and another guest noticed the strong odor of pipe tobacco at dinner one night. No one was smoking.

Accompanied by my friend Frank and psychic Sue Tracy, I drove over to Gallatin Gateway on a hot afternoon in August. The parking lot was crowded, and I was glad I had called ahead for reservations. All the rooms in the main building had been booked for a convention, so we had been assigned comfortable lodging in one of the nearby cottages. When we checked in, I asked about the inn's ghosts and was promptly referred to one of the housekeepers, a pleasant woman who had worked there for nearly two decades. She readily agreed to talk to me but preferred to remain anonymous.

First, I asked the woman whether there was anything to the legend of the murdered girl. "Oh, yes," she replied with conviction. Her mother had been young at the time of the tragedy and had heard all about it. Apparently a young girl from "somewhere back East" had come out to work at the inn for the summer and fallen in love with one of the waiters. When autumn came and it was time to close down for the winter, the girl told a friend that she wouldn't be going back with the rest of them. The friend assumed that the girl had made other arrangements to get home, and left with the other seasonal employees.

A couple of week later, the girl's father contacted the innkeepers. His daughter had not returned home. The worried father came out to Montana and, with others, searched the dorm in which his daughter had stayed. They found no one. The searchers then turned to the inn itself. Room by room they went through the building, finding nothing but sheets and bedding left neatly folded on each bed.

There are two versions of what happened next. Some say that the girl's body was found beneath a heap of bedding on the floor of Room 207. Others claim that her body wasn't found until spring, when staff began to get the inn ready for opening day. According to this version, the body had been hidden in the closet of Room 207. Rumor had it that the girl was pregnant, and may have been smothered by her lover.

Had anything odd been noticed in that room since then? "Well," our informant told us, "I used to clean Room 207 and never felt uneasy in the room, although other maids claimed they did." The girl's ghost had never been seen, as far as she knew.

She then went on to tell us about a male ghost that had been seen on an early winter's day in 1990. "One of the housemaids was taking bedding from the north wing down to the laundry," she said. "She happened to glance across the lounge toward the south wing and saw a man dressed in a black tux standing on the landing. She thought nothing of it, just smiled, nodded to him, and went on about her business. When she asked later, she was told that no one matching that description was staying at the inn. In fact, no one was staying in the south wing at all, since the rooms were being painted."

I thanked the woman for taking time to talk with us. We were ready to explore the beautiful Gallatin Gateway Inn. We admired the huge lounge and fireplace, and took a number of photos of the stairway where the ghostly tuxedoed gentleman had been seen. The grand foyer was impressive, and the veranda, now glassed in and called the Colonnade, held an indefinable air of the 1920s. It was easy to imagine the excited chatter of tourists about to board buses for Yellowstone.

The three of us had dinner that evening in the restaurant. Midway through dinner, both Frank and I became aware of a strong scent of pipe smoke next to us, even though no one was smoking in the restaurant. The windows were open, so Frank got up and went outside to see if anyone was smoking near the windows. No one was there. The smoke was only noticeable in a small area between Frank and me. Sue, our psychic friend from Oregon, was seated across from us and did not smell the pipe tobacco. Instead, she caught a whiff of perfume that she described as "floral."

We all passed an undisturbed night. The next morning we enjoyed breakfast in the Colonnade, then made our way through the foyer to the back entrance. We went outside, pausing at the top of the steps to admire the view of the Spanish Peaks Primitive Area in the distance. The morning was already warm, promising another hot day to come. No one else was within sight.

"Where's the lady with the perfume?" I asked Sue, jokingly. All of a sudden the perfume was back, and this time all three of us smelled it. The fragrance seemed very real, a lovely, expensive floral scent concentrated in a small area at the bottom of the steps. We could step into and out of the scent. It lasted several minutes before fading away.

We were stunned by what had happened. There seemed to be no natural explanation. We were outside, in fresh cool air. That scent couldn't possibly be explained as a lingering odor in a stuffy room. And why had it returned just then, moments after I had referred to it? Had one of the ghosts wanted to make her presence known? It was an unsettling thought, to be sure.

Could we have just had a mass hallucination? I had once

asked the then-head of the psychology department at the University of Minnesota what the odds were of a mass hallucination occurring. He estimated the odds at one in ten to the ten millionth—in other words, almost impossible. We already knew there was no rational explanation. If a mass hallucination was ruled out, then we had to conclude that one of the inn's ghosts had just paid us a visit.

Was it the ghost of the murdered girl? That lovely expensive floral scent didn't seem the type of perfume that would have appealed to a young woman. It was more likely to have been worn by an older, more sophisticated woman. And so far there's no proof that a murder even occurred, though the story was apparently well-known to those living in the area at the time.

And who was the man in the black tux seen in 1990? Was he somehow involved in the murder, if murder there was? Waiters in elegant hotels often wore tuxes, at least in the early part of the century. Could this man have been one of the waiters, perhaps the one reputed to have been the girl's lover? Was he also responsible for the strong odor of pipe smoke that Frank and I had noticed?

Of course, the lady who wore expensive perfume and the gentleman who smoked a pipe may have had nothing to do with a murder. After all, thousands of guests must have stayed at the inn during its heyday. Perhaps the ghostly lady and her escort were simply a well-to-do couple who had enjoyed their stay so much that they decided to remain… forever. Glancing back at the inn in its romantic setting as we drove away, I couldn't blame them.

The Gallatin Gateway Inn has an indefinable aura of the past. It's easy to imagine the excited bustle of crowds as the trains arrived and departed, and perhaps that's part of the charm of this beautiful inn. If you're fortunate, you may catch the elusive scent of expensive perfume or a whiff of pipe smoke when no one else is around.

HONKY-TONK TIME
IN GARNET

GARNET GHOST TOWN
c/o Garnet Preservation Association
3255 Fort Missoula Road
Missoula, Montana 59804
406-329-3883

Ghostly Activity Level: Moderate

HISTORY: Garnet was founded in 1895 to process gold from the nearby Nancy Hanks mine. When gold became scarce, however, the population dropped rapidly from its peak of about 1,000. A fire in 1912 burned many of the buildings and most inhabitants left town. As late as the 1960s there were only a few summer residents. Although a mining town, Garnet was never as lawless as Bannack or Virginia City, perhaps because most of the miners brought their families. The remaining wooden buildings have been stabilized but not restored. Access is by road during summer and by ski or snowmobile in winter. The ghost town of Garnet is owned and managed by the Bureau of Land Management, assisted by the Garnet Preservation Association.

PHENOMENA: Honky-tonk piano music, voices, and clinking glasses were heard coming from Kelly's Saloon by Garnet's winter caretakers. They also reported unexplained footsteps in the J. K. Wells Hotel. Visitors who rent one of the cabins in winter sometimes report seeing figures wearing old-fashioned clothing who vanish before their eyes. Strange figures sometimes show up in photographs taken in various buildings.

Our first visit to Garnet could well have been our last. I wasn't used to mountain driving at the time, but Frank had spent much of his boyhood exploring the mountains around Lewistown and was completely at home on even the worst roads. When he confidently directed me to turn onto Bear Creek Road I did so, unaware of the route's reputation. A section of this steep, narrow, dirt road called China Grade has seemingly been carved out of the side of a cliff. If another vehicle had been coming down one of us would have had to back up in hopes of finding a slightly wider spot to pull into. Worse, there was a drop of what looked like hundreds of feet on the driver's side and a steep embankment on the other side. When my Buick nearly high-centered on a large rock I couldn't take it anymore. While ghosts don't scare me, China Grade emphatically did!

"*You* drive," I told Frank, and eased out of the car, all too aware of the dropoff less than a yard away. He shifted into the driver's seat and drove carefully up the road while I trudged behind on foot, as far from the edge of the road as I could get. When we finally reached the top and saw Garnet, we noticed several other cars arriving from another direction and realized that there must be a different, and presumably less dangerous, way to reach Garnet.

My legs were shaking after my ordeal, so I found a cool spot beneath a pine tree and sat to rest while Frank parked the car. I was aware that Garnet was supposed to be haunted, of course, but I was still too unnerved to think about ghosts.

The breeze soughing through the pine trees above me was relaxing, and I soon began to take an interest in the town spread out below me. Almost immediately something struck me as odd: although the breeze was now strong enough to create a tossing sea of pine branches at the edge of town, the tall grasses around the buildings weren't moving at all. There was an unnatural stillness about the place that I thought I recognized. A few people were strolling around the log buildings and occasionally I could hear the laughter of children splashing in a tiny creek, but it all seemed superficial, just a ripple on the surface of a deep pool of time. I'd encountered that phenomenon once before, on Bosworth Field in England, where King Richard III had lost his life and crown. The crest of the hill where the king and his supporters had made camp had been absolutely silent, the grasses unmoving, although the trees at the edge of the hill were swaying in a strong breeze. Even our guide had commented on it.

Perhaps Garnet, like haunted Bosworth, wasn't quite dead after all.

I tried to imagine what Garnet must be like in winter. The only way to reach the town would be by ski or snowmobile. There would be no shouts of little children running about, no distant crunch of cars on gravel, just the sigh of the wind and an occasional thump as a snow cornice dropped from the roof of one of the old log buildings. And at night, under the burning stars, perhaps the gay tinkle of honky-tonk music from Kelly's Saloon, or the sharp rap of invisible fingers on a caretaker's cabin door in the darkness.

The stories can be traced back to at least the early 1970s. Many of them describe unexplained footsteps on the second floor of the J. K. Wells Hotel, probably the most impressive building still standing in Garnet. The hotel was built in 1897 and closed in the 1930s. The building was considered elegant for its time, with carved wood doors, stained-glass windows, and an oak staircase.

John Ellingsen of the Montana Heritage Commission spent considerable time at Garnet in various capacities from 1970 to 1972. "In 1970 I was a volunteer representing the Montana Historical Society," he told me. "I had never heard any stories about the ghosts before then. One day I happened to be taking measurements in the J. K. Wells Hotel. A friend's dog was with me. I heard footsteps coming from the empty second floor of the hotel. The dog, who was probably more sensitive than I was, appeared terrified and ran out of the building. It was broad daylight, probably in late July. After that I always got the shivers whenever I was walking around town making sure things were all right, especially at night. I've been back to Garnet several times since then, but I've never had another ghostly experience there."

Ellingsen was the first of several people to report paranormal activity at Garnet in the 1970s. One of the most dramatic occurrences happened to his friend, Mike Gordon, who was hired by the Bureau of Land Management to be the guard in the winter. According to Ellingsen, Gordon heard music playing in Kelly's Saloon one night in the dead of winter.

"It was like they were having a wild party down there, with piano playing, people singing," Ellingsen quoted Gordon as saying. "When Mike went out to see what was going on, the music stopped and the place was completely dark."

Four carpenters from Glacier National Park who were brought in to stabilize one of the rotting cabins in Garnet also experienced something uncanny at Garnet. According to an article entitled "History Channel Films as Carpenters Wrap Up Garnet Preservation Project" in the *Missoulian* of October 27, 2002, construction materials sometimes could not be found when needed, and tools set down briefly were missing an instant later. "That's my story and I'm sticking to it," Dave Eubank, head of the park's special projects group, was quoted as saying. "Now it's gotten to the point that whenever anything happens, it's the ghost. *We* never make mistakes." Eubanks may have spoken tongue-in-cheek, but the eerie occurrences happened too often to be explained as absentmindedness on the part of four experienced carpenters.

A number of photographs taken at Garnet have revealed more than was visible to the photographer's eye at the time. A Great Falls woman reported that she found several ghostly images on a photo she had taken in the hotel. Another visitor claimed to have photographed what looked like a tall, thin, shadowy figure in the old blacksmith shop.

Odd things continue to happen. Janet Goodsell is a volunteer from New York who has spent one month each summer since 2000 greeting people in the visitor center. She had an odd experience in August 2004, on Friday the thirteenth. "A visitor to Garnet came down to the visitor center after roaming over the hill to look at the miners' cabins that are still standing," Goodsell related. "She brought a digital camera picture to show me a picture of a calendar that was lying on the cookstove next to the door of one of the cabins. It was a tear-off calendar page from August 1943. Coincidentally, August of 1943 also had a Friday the thirteenth. Our historian, Allen Mathews, also saw the photo.

"I immediately went up the hill to confirm the existence of the page, and it was lying on the stove as reported. There were no additional visitors in town, and since by then it was closing time we locked up the buildings so Allen could walk up the hill to see this calendar for himself. When he got there, it was gone. We believe there were no other people in town, and we know there was no one else who heard the conversation about the calendar."

Garnet seems to have classic examples of residual haunting, in which emotional energies are supposedly absorbed by stone or wooden buildings or by concentrations of minerals in the vicinity. It's thought that occasionally, when someone who is sensitive enough is close by, he or she will hear or see a replay of an event that occurred long ago. The "ghosts" in a case of residual haunting do not react to an observer and are actually a sort of recorded image. Typically, when an observer gets too close, their own electromagnetic field interferes with the replay and the "ghostly" sounds stop abruptly.

The Garnet Mountains are full of minerals, particularly quartz, which is known to amplify and store energy, so the residual haunting theory seems the most likely explanation for most of the odd events that have occurred at Garnet.

If you enjoy solitude in winter and would like to rent one of the cabins at Garnet, don't be surprised to hear ghostly music from Kelly's Saloon, for although paranormal activity is reported at all seasons, the town seems to come eerily alive after most tourists have gone. Should you attempt to investigate, however, the music will most likely cut off instantly. All that will be left will be the intense winter cold and the darkness.

A FLASH
OF BLUE

TRACY'S 24-HOUR FAMILY RESTAURANT
127 Central Avenue
Great Falls, Montana 59401
406-453-6108

Ghostly Activity Level: Low

HISTORY: The first building on the site where Tracy's now stands was the Stanton Bank & Trust, established around 1918. The bank closed its doors in 1923, bankrupt after loaning $73,000 to the promoters of the financially ruinous Dempsey-Gibbons prize fight held in Shelby. The building eventually burned down. In 1938 Hank's Hamburger Haven was built on the old foundation. Hank's became Louie's Kitchenette, and in 1952 Tracy Redeau leased the restaurant and changed the name to Tracy's Restaurant. The restaurant is currently owned and operated by the third generation of the Redeau family.

PHENOMENA: Over the years since Tracy Redeau's death several employees of the restaurant have glimpsed someone wearing a blue sweater in the basement or in the dining area. When they turn to take a closer look, no one is there. At times unexplained loud noises are heard from the kitchen.

Tracy Redeau is still keeping a benevolent eye on the restaurant he started in 1952. That would not be at all unusual for a man who is dedicated to his work—except that Tracy Redeau died in 1981.

According to an article in the *Great Falls Tribune* published on June 19, 2003, Tracy's son Jim Redeau stated that two employees claimed to have seen a figure resembling "Mr. Tracy" in the restaurant, and that a cook was afraid to go downstairs because he'd seen Tracy in the basement. One of the waitresses told Jim she had seen a blurry figure wearing a blue sweater in the kitchen. She had never met Tracy and did not know that he habitually wore a blue sweater to work.

Jim Redeau died shortly after that article was written, and ownership of the restaurant passed to Tracy Redeau's grandson, Nick Redeau, and his wife Veronica. I met the young couple when I stopped in to ask whether "Mr. Tracy" had been seen lately. I mentioned that on a previous visit, one of the waitresses had told me that she sometimes heard loud crashes and bangs from the kitchen, and that the employees jokingly blame them on "Tracy." Nick acknowledged that he had heard the story, but was cautious about attributing the noises to his grandfather's spirit. He pointed out that there was a lot of mechanical equipment in the kitchen that kicked on periodically, causing loud noises that could be mistaken for the clattering of pots and pans.

He doesn't discount all the stories about his grandfather's ghost, however. "The basement was where the cook had the first sighting of Grandpa's ghost," Nick said. "I spend a lot of time in the basement, and I haven't seen anything yet. Maybe I'm trying too hard." The basement is used primarily for storage.

Nick and Veronica did a lot of historical research about

the property before they bought the restaurant. Underground tunnels formerly ran between buildings in the area and, according to Nick, one tunnel led into the basement. The tunnels have all been filled in over the years, though.

"I was only three when Grandpa passed away," Nick said. "He came from Chicago originally. He ran the restaurant for twenty-three years and my dad, Jim Redeau, ran it for twenty-nine. I've been working here since I was thirteen, washing dishes and fixing stuff. I bought the place when I was twenty-six, after my dad died. We want to carry on the family legacy. Hopefully someday we'll have a kid who'll want to take over."

Veronica may have glimpsed Tracy's ghost one night. She said, "The closest I came was right after we first bought the restaurant. We had a waitress who didn't show up one night so I had to cover the night shift. I swear I saw something walk into the bathroom. When I told Nick, he asked if it'd been wearing a blue shirt. I don't know if I actually saw something or if it was from being tired."

She wasn't the first to have that experience. Several of the waitresses have seen a blue streak out of the corners of their eyes when nobody else is in the restaurant, according to Nick. "They'll come out to see who came into the restaurant and there won't be anyone there. When the waitresses described the blue flash they didn't even know grandpa wore a blue sweater. It got my dad's attention real quick. They didn't think anything of it, but he did, because he had worked down here with my grandpa and saw him day in and day out, usually wearing a blue sweater or sweatshirt."

Nick recalled something eerie. "A few hours after my grandpa passed away, my dad got a phone call that all the electric signs that said 'Tracy's' had quit working down here. It was kind of odd. The same thing happened when my dad passed away. My signs started acting up. All the flashers quit working on the blue breakers. It got my attention for sure. It didn't really hit me until I was up there tinkering with it and got the breakers reset, and then I remembered my dad's story. I've never had a problem with it since, and those signs are on every day and night."

Tracy's Restaurant is open 24 hours a day and affectionately regarded as a Great Falls institution. Nick and Veronica have modernized where necessary, but were careful not to destroy the retro look of the diner. The menu is straight out of the 1950s, and photos from the 1940s and 1950s line the walls. You can choose to sit on stools at the counter, or in a wall booth complete with tabletop jukeboxes that work. Tracy's was featured in the film *Holy Matrimony*, starring Leonard Nimoy, filmed in Great Falls in 1993.

Tracy's Restaurant is a nostalgic experience for those of us who grew up in the 1950s. Why not drop a quarter in one of the jukeboxes while you look over the extensive menu of hearty offerings? Don't miss the vibrantly colored tiles in the ladies' washroom (Veronica says that even the gents can take a peek when it's not in use). If you happen to see a blurry figure wearing a blue sweater passing by, just smile and nod—it's only "Mr. Tracy" keeping an eye on things.

MYSTERY AT
THE MUSEUM

PARIS GIBSON SQUARE MUSEUM OF ART
1400 First Avenue North
Great Falls, Montana 59401
406-727-8255

Ghostly Activity Level: Moderate

HISTORY: This magnificent building was the first high school in Cascade County. Completed in 1896, it was named Central High School. In 1939, after a second high school was built, Central was renamed Paris Gibson Junior High School after the man who founded the city of Great Falls. The aging building was closed in 1975 but reopened by volunteers in 1977 as the Paris Gibson Square Museum of Art. The building is made of local gray sandstone. The walls are four to five feet thick and extend 16 feet deep to reach bedrock.

PHENOMENA: Several staff members working in the museum have experienced the sounds of rattling keys, a man's voice, kids getting out of school, and a feeling of being watched by someone invisible. The haunting may be connected to a drowning in the school swimming pool in 1915.

For many years I've heard rumors about a teenage boy who reputedly drowned in a swimming pool in the basement of the school that is now Paris Gibson Square Museum of Art. Details vary, but the most common version is that the boy's friends pushed him into the water as a prank. The boy couldn't swim, and the prank turned deadly. The accident was supposedly covered up by school authorities because there were no lifeguards on duty at the time. Soon after that the pool was permanently closed.

Local reporter Carol Bradley decided to track down the real story, aided by local historians and museum staff. The result was the article "Ghost Busting at PGS," published by the *Great Falls Tribune* on June 13, 1999. In an impressive piece of investigative journalism, Bradley succeeded in uncovering the origins of a story that had nearly attained urban legend status.

An alumnus of Central High School, Art Beecher, who graduated in 1919, recalled that the rumors were current in his school days. He also stated that the victim's father sold John Deere farm implements. Beecher was certain of that much because his parents and the parents of the boy who drowned were acquainted.

A search of old city directories quickly revealed a listing for an implement dealer who sold John Deere tractors: George G. Mill. That led to Mill's obituary in 1952, which mentioned a son, Grant Mill, who had died in Great Falls in 1916. High school yearbooks confirmed that Grant Webber Mill had indeed been a member of the class of 1916 at Central High School, though cemetery records indicate he drowned on October 16, 1915, not 1916. The site of the drowning was the Missouri River, not the high school swimming pool.

Newspaper microfilm from October 15, 1915, revealed the details of the long-forgotten accident. Mill, who was terrified of water and could not swim, had gone boating with three friends. Somehow he fell off the houseboat and went under.

His body was located several hours later by the sheriff and several other searchers.

Unless the sheriff and everyone else involved in the search agreed to take part in a widespread cover-up, Grant Mill did not drown at the high school. And he most certainly did not drown in a pool in the boiler room, because according to newspaper articles the pool was located in an annex built in 1913. The pool developed cracks that could not be repaired and was closed in 1917, although the annex itself existed until 1975.

Despite Bradley's impressive research, the legend of the drowning persists—and so does a haunting, according to Kathy Lear, Executive Director of the Paris Gibson Square Museum of Art. She confirmed by e-mail that several members of the staff had encountered a ghost, and that the haunting may be linked to the drowning victim.

I wanted to find out more, so I drove up to Great Falls with my friends Frank and Sue. Lear and marketing director Deborah Shore greeted us; both have had eerie experiences in the building. We toured the beautifully restored building from the attic to the boiler room, which rumor still insists was the site of the former pool. The room certainly looked as if it could once have held a deep rectangular pool. Unlike modern pools, a pool of that era would have been of even depth, with no shallow end for those who were poor swimmers.

I had been taping Lear's commentary as we toured the building and at that point invited the spirit of Grant Mill, should he be present, to make his presence known. Ghostly voices have occasionally been captured on audiotape, a phenomenon called "electronic voice phenomena," or EVP. When I replayed the tape, however, the only voice on the tape belonged to Kathy Lear.

If the drowning victim doesn't haunt the school he once

attended, who does? There's little doubt that the old building *is* haunted. A number of employees and volunteers over the years have reported some very odd experiences. One of them was a young woman who had just graduated and was offered a job at the school.

Lear told me, "She always felt like someone was standing by her desk looking at her. He seemed to be a male authority figure, telling her what to do. She could not leave the building at night. Whenever she would punch her code into the security system, weird things would happen, like it would show a door ajar. When she would go check, the door wouldn't be ajar. She used to get so upset about checking out that one night I left with her. She put her code in four times and got all these errors that said 'go check this room, go check that room.' When I put my code in, it was fine.

"One night she was getting ready to leave and she heard a male voice say, 'Get out!' When she tried to leave she couldn't. That's why she never wanted to code out."

Perhaps the authority figure the young woman sensed enjoyed using his power to intimidate people. Or perhaps he was simply lonely. In either case, when I replayed my audiotape the next day, I found that at this point it had picked up an agitated male voice that said, 'She could hear me!'

Lear may have encountered the authoritative male ghost as well. "I was working late one evening after an exhibition reception up on the first floor, cleaning up dishes and stuff. All my office mates had left and the lights were off when I realized that my purse was locked in my office on the second floor. There was nobody I could call to let me back into my office so I called the building superintendent. He lived a little ways away and said he'd be there in fifteen or twenty minutes.

"I waited by the reception desk in front of the gallery. We

had a public telephone at the time and I saw the flasher light up, indicating a call, so I answered it. It was my husband. He had expected me home earlier. I was explaining to him what had happened when behind me I heard a loud 'Hrumph!' It was a male clearing his voice very loudly about two or three feet away. I turned around and nobody was there. I said to my husband, 'Wait, I heard something.' I thought it was the building super who had come in quietly and was waiting for me to notice him. I dragged the phone over so I could look down the stairs and the base flipped and disconnected from my husband.

"I didn't realize it had hung up on him, so I was still holding the handset and saying, 'It must have been the ghost, ha ha,' but all my husband had heard was 'I'm alone in the building. Wait, I think I hear something.' Then *click,* and the phone went dead. He called back right away and then the super came in and I made him clear the building with me again. There was no one here."

Deborah Shore had a strange story, too. "I was down here all by myself in the building," she began. "It was nine-thirty or ten at night. All of a sudden I started hearing a noisy din, like a bunch of happy kids getting off school. I said to myself, 'Okay, there are kids here and I need to figure out what they're doing.' I looked all around. It was late at night, in winter, and there was no one around. I came back and the same thing happened. I looked all the way around and there was no sign of any life."

Perhaps what Deborah Shore heard that night was a residual haunting, the result of energies given off by schoolchildren over the nearly 80 years the building was used as a school. The theory is that energy can be absorbed by the fabric of a building, particularly one built of stone. When conditions are right and a sensitive person is nearby, sounds from the past are replayed. The sounds are actual, not subjective, and in some cases have been recorded.

That theory doesn't explain the encounters with the male authority figure. Although most incidents involving him have occurred on the main floor, he has also made his presence known in the basement. According to Shore, other ladies who worked at the museum and were responsible for clearing the building reported that when they reached the basement they would often hear keys rattle. If, as Lear and Shore are inclined to believe, he was a former principal or teacher, he would undoubtedly have been carrying a set of keys. Another staff member who has an office in the basement sometimes senses a different ghost wandering around her office, this one a 17-year-old blonde girl.

Why does the male authority figure linger long after his death? Is there a connection between him and the blonde girl in the basement? The more we find out, the more confusing it all becomes. The only thing we can be reasonably certain of is that drowning victim Grant Mill does not haunt his former school. He, it seems, has graduated from the school of life and gone onward.

Paris Gibson Square Museum of Art is worth visiting, for the exhibits as well as for its architecture and the sense of history enclosed in its walls. At Christmas they showcase a wonderful bazaar. Don't be surprised if you hear a loud "hrumph!" behind you and turn to find no one there. Apparently some people don't know when it's time to retire.

THE GHOST OF BLACK HORSE LAKE

BLACK HORSE LAKE
Highway 87, near mile-marker 9
North of Great Falls, Montana

Ghostly Activity Level: Low

HISTORY: Local histories of Cascade County barely mention Black Horse Lake, except to say that there were large Indian encampments in the area. The lake is shallow and usually dry, located in a low reedy area to the west of Highway 87 about nine miles north of Great Falls.

PHENOMENA: Since the 1970s, the ghost of a man described as a Native American wearing jeans and a jean jacket or, alternatively, a man in bib overalls, has been seen late at night on Highway 87 near Black Horse Lake. The apparition materializes in the middle of the road so quickly that drivers have no chance to avoid it. Sometimes they feel a thud as if their car has actually struck a person. When they stop to search for the victim, no one is ever found.

A number of encounters with the ghost of Black Horse Lake have been reported over the years, but most of the stories are third-hand. When I visited Fort Benton, however, I was introduced by ghost researcher Mary Doerk to Mrs. Sadie Lippert, one of a number of people who had shared an incredible experience near the notorious Black Horse Lake years ago. I was astounded to hear from Mrs. Lippert that *ten* people in two cars had seen what must have been a ghost in 1973. The memory of what they experienced has remained sharp over the years, although only a few are still willing to talk about it.

According to Mrs. Lippert, she and nine others from Fort Benton had driven to Great Falls to celebrate a March wedding anniversary. Mrs. Lippert's husband Bob drove one car, carrying Mrs. Lippert, her daughter, and two others. A local doctor drove the second car, with four passengers.

Late that evening the doctor received an urgent call to return to Fort Benton. It was about 10:30, fully dark when the two cars left Great Falls. The trip normally takes about 45 minutes, and most of the group had made the drive many times. No one could have predicted that a routine excursion would turn into a voyage into the twilight zone.

The Lipperts' car was in the lead, the second car not far behind. As they started down the hill toward Black Horse Lake, their headlights illuminated a long stretch of empty road. Without warning, the figure of a Native American man appeared spread-eagled on the windshield of the Lipperts' car.

"He was maybe in his thirties or forties," Mrs. Lippert recalled. "His hair was blowing way back. He was just *there*. We didn't hear a thump. We heard nothing—he was just on our windshield. I can still picture it today. He had a red bandana with a little white on it tied around his head. He had a jean jacket on, and his mouth was open in a scream. I remember seeing his teeth. We couldn't see his legs. He flew over our car and landed on the windshield of the car behind us in exactly the same manner. Everyone in the two cars saw him.

"I said to Bob, 'Stop, we hit somebody!' and he said 'No, there's no blood.' He did slow down, but we didn't stop. The second car did stop. The doctor got out and called, 'Where are you? I'm a doctor. I can help you.' No one answered. There was nothing there. When we got to Carter, we called the Highway Patrol. They went back and searched. There was nothing. Everybody was so upset. We talked about it for a long, long time afterward.

"A lot of them won't talk about it now, but my daughter stopped by yesterday and I was telling her, and she said, 'Oh, I'll never forget that!'"

For a moment those of us listening to Mrs. Lippert's horrifying story were silent, perhaps visualizing the sudden frightful appearance of the man on the windshield. Then Mrs. Lippert added quietly, "I still won't go through there at night alone."

So many odd things happened while I was collecting stories for this book that I was hardly surprised when, three months after I had talked to Mrs. Lippert, another eyewitness unexpectedly surfaced. The young man had originally lived in Great Falls with his mother, before moving to Florida. After his mother's death, he moved to Billings and heard that I was interested in Montana ghost stories.

"Have you heard about the ghost of Black Horse Lake?" he asked. I nodded and quickly grabbed a pen to make notes.

"I had an experience one night in the fall of 1995," he began. "I was driving up Highway 87 on the way to Havre to pick up a friend. I had just passed Black Horse Lake when I caught a glimpse of a man wearing some sort of jacket walking along the side of the road with his back to me. There was no oncoming traffic so I moved over to the other lane to give him plenty of room. Suddenly it felt like my car hit something. I saw something flash past the windshield, got maybe a momentary glimpse of a face, and pulled over to the shoulder as quickly as I could. As soon as I got the car stopped, I got out and started looking around to see what I had hit. I didn't think I had hit the man I saw, but maybe a deer or something. A Highway Patrol officer came by a few minutes later and stopped. I told him what had happened. He got out a powerful flashlight and helped me look for whatever it was I had hit. We couldn't find anything, either deer or human. I remember the weather was clear and it was full dark at the time. The next day I checked my car to see if there was any damage but there was none."

According to Mrs. Lippert, none of the many eyewitnesses in the two cars had ever heard of a fatal accident involving a pedestrian and a car at this location, nor had the young man who encountered the ghost in 1995. Unless someone stumbles across an account of a fatality in that area in old newspaper microfilms, we'll probably never know who the victim was.

Stay alert if you drove north on Highway 87 after dark, particularly as you approach Black Horse Lake. And don't breathe a sigh of relief until you're well past, for you may be the next driver to see the ghost of a screaming man flattened against your windshield.

A SCENT
OF ROSES

MARCUS DALY NATIONAL HISTORIC SITE
251 Eastside Highway
Hamilton, Montana 59840
406-363-6004

Ghostly Activity Level: Moderate

HISTORY: The mansion "Riverside" was built in 1896 by "copper king" Marcus Daly as a summer residence. Daly's financial empire included the Anaconda smelter, banks, and livestock breeding farms. He waged a bitter political war with fellow copper king William A. Clark, a feud enlivened by charges of bribery and corruption on both sides. Daly died in 1900 at age 58. Between 1906 and 1910 his widow, Margaret, had the mansion rebuilt in a Georgian Revival style. She returned there each summer until her death in 1941. The mansion remained empty, gradually deteriorating, until 1987, when it was opened to the public. It now is owned by the state of Montana and operated by the Daly Mansion Preservation Trust.

PHENOMENA: The scent of roses has been noticed in summer around the time of Margaret Daly's birthday. Volunteers sometimes feel as if an invisible person is standing behind them. A prized painting fell repeatedly from the wall until it was placed in the very spot it had originally occupied. Mrs. Daly herself appeared to a descendent of the Chaffin family (the original owners of the property) who was accompanying a group of youngsters through the house. Motion detectors in Margaret's bedroom indicated something was moving about the room, although no one was visible at the time. A young girl told her mother that she could "see" a lady sitting at the table in the dining room, smiling at visitors. The description matched that of Mrs. Daly.

The morning was pleasantly cool when we pulled into the parking lot. A long gravel drive led to the house, barely visible through the trees, and we could hear the distant hum of a lawn tractor somewhere on the grounds. We strolled around the property, trying to imagine what it must have been like to be lord or lady of the manor in the early 1900s. The grounds are impressive, with more than 500 trees, many of them rare species not native to Montana. As well, there is a swimming pool, tennis courts, greenhouse, and the remains of the elaborate stable built for Daly's champion racehorses.

The home is a three-story, 24,000-square-foot mansion with 25 bedrooms and 15 bathrooms. Now listed in the National Register of Historic Places, it replaced an earlier home where the Daly family had spent several happy years. The mansion is gradually being restored, but many of the rooms are still empty. In places, walls have been stripped to lath and plaster, and some of the ceilings show water damage.

We watched a short video about the Daly family and Riverside. Afterward, a knowledgeable volunteer named Elaine gave us a tour of the music room, living room, kitchen, Mr. Daly's office, and the Evans suite, all on the main floor. We were then free to explore the upper floors on our own.

I later returned to the main floor because I had sensed a presence there earlier. In fact, the feeling was so strong that I had momentarily felt I was intruding on someone's privacy. Elaine was between tours at the moment, so she accompanied us back to the Evans suite, reserved for Mrs. Daly's invalid sister, Martha Evans. Miss Evans was quite frail, possibly as a result of polio, and always traveled with a companion. Their bedrooms were on the main floor next to a bathroom. The suite still had most of its original furnishings.

I decided to tell Elaine what I had sensed. She didn't seem at all surprised. The Evans suite's bathroom was now used by the volunteers, and odd things sometimes happened there. "I was in the volunteers' bathroom washing my hands one day," Elaine told us, "and I felt someone behind me. I turned around and no one was there. At the time, I knew none of the ghost stories."

Later, when I played back my audiotape, I heard a faint whisper while Elaine was telling us about her peculiar experience in the volunteers' bathroom. It was definitely a woman's voice, speaking at the same time as Elaine. Only the word "washing" can be made out.

Donna McCrimmon, another volunteer, told us that she had been walking down a hallway alone when she heard someone speak behind her. She turned around to reply but no one was there.

"Did the voice sound male or female?" I asked.

"I don't recall," she replied. "Actually, it was less a sound than a feeling. That's not the only place where odd things have happened though. Ghostbusters set up motion detectors in Mrs. Daly's bedroom and in the hallway where the second-floor sitting room is, where we know she liked to read to the children in the evening. During the night, the detectors indicated that something was moving around in Mrs. Daly's bedroom. When they went upstairs to check, no one was there.

"Another time I smelled roses. Mrs. Daly loved roses, and a lot of people say they smell roses on Mrs. Daly's birthday. This wasn't her birthday, though, and the windows were open, so I probably just smelled the rose garden."

Then McCrimmon showed us a photo that had been taken at a fundraiser on the grounds. The swimming pool had been filled especially for the occasion. The pool had deteriorated over the years and was no longer capable of holding water for more than a few hours, but everyone had a good time while it was full. The photo showed the pool, and a grayish mist with rainbow colors in it hovering above a small building just beyond the pool. There seemed no natural explanation for the mist. Perhaps Mrs. Daly had been pleased to see the pool in use once more, and made her approval known in that manner.

Margaret Daly had strong opinions and did not hesitate to make her disapproval known. McCrimmon recounted the story of one of Mrs. Daly's favorite paintings. The painting, called "Musicale," had originally been displayed in the living room. During restoration, workers hung the painting in the adjacent music room. The next morning it was found lying on the floor, undamaged. Workers hung it back up and the following morning again found it on the floor. They promptly moved it back to its original spot in the living room and it has stayed in place ever since.

Mrs. Daly may not be the only former inhabitant to return in spirit to the house she loved so much. When I replayed the audiotape I had made of the tour, I was surprised to hear an elderly male voice mutter a few indistinct words in the kitchen. Mr. Daly was only 58 when he died, so presumably the voice wasn't his.

The house is currently undergoing massive restoration estimated to cost $2 million. Craftspeople who are specialists in the arts of the Victorian era have been hired, and it's fascinating—though unsettling— to think that the spirit of Margaret Daly may be hovering over their shoulders, watching with a critical eye as they work to bring her beloved house back to its former glory.

"Riverside" and its beautiful grounds are well worth visiting. Don't be surprised if you catch a glimpse of a regal lady standing in the shadows, smiling gently at the pleasure her visitors take in her house.

LITTLE BIGHORN BATTLEFIELD

LITTLE BIGHORN BATTLEFIELD NATIONAL MONUMENT
Crow Agency, Montana 59022
406-638-2621

Ghostly Activity Level: High

HISTORY: On June 25, 1876, 7th Cavalry scouts discovered a huge village of Sioux and Cheyenne Indians camped along the Little Bighorn River. Lieutenant Colonel George Armstrong Custer split his troops, ordering Major Marcus Reno to attack the village while Captain Benteen circled to the southwest. Custer rode north with 210 troops. Reno and his men met fierce resistance and scrambled back to a bluff three miles away, where they and Benteen's returning troops were pinned down by enemy fire. The Indians then turned their attention to Custer. Outnumbered and outfought, Custer and all his men were killed.

The site of the battle, now known as the Little Bighorn Battlefield National Monument, covers 600 acres plus about 160 acres of the Reno-Benteen entrenchment. The land consists of rolling plains cut by deep draws, and is sparsely covered with sagebrush, prickly pear cactus, and bunchgrass. The hill where Custer and many of his troops died in 1876 is near the visitor center; the high ground where Major Reno and his men were besieged is about 4.5 miles away by car. Summer visitors should go early in the morning before the heat becomes excessive, and stay on the paths; rattlesnakes are often seen in the area.

PHENOMENA: Sounds of war whoops and rifle shots from the battlefield are sometimes heard at night. Staff members heard the thud of booted feet in the museum. Tourists, park rangers, and Native Americans living nearby glimpsed figures of Indian warriors on ponies. Rangers living in the Old Stone House (now used for offices) awakened to see the figures of Indians and at least one soldier killed during the battle. A woman visiting for the first time "saw" bodies of soldiers and horses scattered over Custer Hill. The spine-tingling call of a bugle was heard early in the morning by re-enactors camped nearby.

The long shadow of the Custer monument stretched eastward in the evening sunlight as I stood looking back across the battlefield. Most visitors had already left and the battlefield seemed eerily quiet. No insects buzzed, no birds sang, and even the warm breeze had died away. I couldn't help but wonder if it had felt like this on June 27, 1876, when Brigadier General Terry's troopers rode up to find Custer, his men, and most of their horses lying dead and bloated under a searing hot sun.

For a moment the amenities of home seemed all too far away, and the ghosts of Little Bighorn Battlefield all too close.

The troops who rode with Custer had not expected to die that hot June day in 1876. Unlike the men who died at Concord Bridge, at Valley Forge, at Gettysburg, most were not fighting for a cherished cause. Many were recent immigrants who had come to this country to find a new life. Instead, they found a particularly gruesome death. According to many reports, their anguished spirits may still linger where they died.

Custer himself is said to haunt the visitor center. A number of items that once belonged to him are displayed there, and many more are stored in the basement. The sounds of heavy booted footsteps have been heard at times, and employees have reportedly glimpsed a ghostly figure who resembles General Custer.

Another soldier's ghost was seen at the Old Stone House when it was still used as housing for staff. One night a ranger awoke to see the image of a soldier in her room. The expression of fear and anguish on his face impressed her so much that the next day she looked at photos of Custer's troops to try to identify him. He was Lt. Benjamin Hodgson, killed as he tried to scramble up the banks of the Little Bighorn River at Reno Crossing.

Visitors have recorded chilling sounds on audiotape at various places on the battlefield. One woman discovered that her tape recorder had captured a man's hoarse scream of agony just outside the visitor center. Others have recorded what sounds like voices singing or chanting in unfamiliar languages, perhaps Sioux. On rare occasions the sounds of battle were heard by the human ear.

A college professor who spent many summers working as a ranger at the battlefield told me of the ghostly soldiers seen by many of his colleagues, and of the whoops and yells and the gunshots carried down the wind from nowhere that he had heard more than once. One night he and a companion actually barricaded themselves in their quarters because they had glimpsed shadowy forms moving on the hill where Custer died.

Robert Lampe of Butte heard inexplicable sounds apparently from the past. Lampe often participates in the annual re-enactment of the battle. A career soldier, he is not easily spooked, but in June 2002 he had an experience he will not easily forget. "My brother and I arrived the Sunday prior to the reenactment and set up our camp along the banks of the Little Bighorn River, on property owned by the Real Bird family who are the producers of the re-enactment," he recalled. "One morning I awoke about three A.M. with the need to visit the porta-potty, which was quite a distance from our camp. After getting out of my nice warm bed and getting dressed, I began the walk to the porta-potty. About halfway there I began to hear a bugle. At first I thought I was just hearing things, and then it started again. I stopped to listen and discerned that it was coming from the direction of Last Stand Hill, where the monument now stands.

"For some reason this bugle sounded different, as it was in a different key than modern bugles and had a sort of hollow sound to it. It kept playing the same bugle call over and over… that call was 'Recall.' I figured it was somebody playing a practical joke on me and continued on my way.

"The next morning I asked a real lieutenant colonel at the reenactment just who was sounding the bugle the previous night. He smiled and asked, 'Where was it coming from?' When I told him Last Stand Hill, he turned absolutely white and began nodding his head in the affirmative. He then informed me that there was not a bugle within five miles of where we were, that the park closes at nine P.M. and no one is allowed in after that until eight o'clock the next morning. He further explained that I am not the only person to have heard this 'ghostly trumpeter' [in 1876 they were called trumpeters, not buglers] and I more than likely will not be the last. He also told me that in all likelihood it is the ghost of Custer's trumpeter Henry Voss sounding 'Recall' in the hopes that Reno and Benteen will come to the rescue with their combined force of about three hundred men."

Lampe concluded his tale with, "Chief Trumpeter Voss will be sounding 'Recall' for the rest of eternity or until Reno and Benteen finally do come to the rescue."

Does the spirit of Voss, one of the many immigrants who died with Custer that day, haunt the battlefield, or is the sound of the bugle a residual haunting, a relic of the battle that was somehow absorbed by the surroundings and replayed when a sufficiently sensitive person happens to be close by? Whatever the answer, Voss is reported to have fought well. His heroic efforts won the admiration of Cheyenne Chief Two Moon, who commented long after the battle, "All along the bugler kept blowing his commands. He was very brave too."

Seattle resident Marilyn Grace visited the battlefield in the mid-1960s. She and her husband arrived late one hot August day just as the park was closing. The ranger allowed her to look around while he finished up his chores. Something totally expected happened: her present-day surroundings faded away and, to her horror, she saw the battlefield as it had been on that fateful day in 1876.

Grace reported: "The yellow-brown grasses were bending under a hot breeze, and the scene took shape for me. First I heard the groans and the whooshes of air being expelled from the injured horses. Some made a coughing sound. And I saw the blood of the horses. Some were lying on injured men who were struggling to get out from under such weight.

"I seem to recall at least three mules downed and dying with leather knapsacks and what I think were metal boxes strapped to their backs. The bellies of two horses were ripped and the horses' back legs struggled. Their eyes looked outward and were not yet glazed over. I felt a sadness come over me for animals looking for masters to rescue them, and an anger.

"Some men seemed to be turning tail and running rather than standing their ground. Some were silent, others screamed with the fear of death. They had not been prepared for a real fight. They thought that they would be back in the taverns to tell the story. Most of the men were not wearing uniforms.

"Indian warriors were falling along with their horses but not running. The Indian women and children were close. But that doesn't seem right when I think of how it must have happened. The ranger joined us and spoke of the ghosts in a half-believing, half-denying tone. I cannot imagine anyone not having their own experience there."

Did Grace have a momentary glimpse into the past? With the exception of the mules, which would most likely have remained with Reno rather than the fast-moving Custer, her account seems accurate. Certainly its impact has remained with her to this day.

Major Reno's spirit is reported to linger near his tombstone in the cemetery behind the visitor center. He was harshly criticized after the battle for not going to Custer's aid, even though he and his men were pinned on a bluff by an overwhelming force of Indians. The injustice still rankles, according to Texas psychic Pat Cody, who visited the battlefield in 1999.

Cody knew little about the battle, but while exploring the cemetery she felt somehow drawn to Reno's tombstone. Suddenly she became aware of a presence in an old-fashioned military uniform. "They kill me yet again," "Reno" complained to her, apparently referring to his burial between two veterans of World War II. He wanted to be buried with his own men instead. Cody tried to explain that he needed to let go of his bitterness in order to move on, but he seemed belligerent and unwilling to listen. Disgruntled, he walked away from her and disappeared.

Spirits of Indian warriors also are seen at the battlefield. Many must have gone willingly to meet death, fighting to preserve a way of life that was already passing into history. A memorial to those warriors now stands at the battlefield.

The Reno-Benteen entrenchment area also has its ghosts. At times there is a feeling of tense expectancy so strong that the hair literally stands up on the back of one's neck. A historical re-enactor who spends most of his summers at Virginia City still recalls the dark, cloudy figure that rushed past him and vanished. Psychic Pat Cody may have sensed the same man, a soldier who staggered past her, nearly demented with thirst. Was he an actual spirit, or merely an imprint left by one of Reno's troopers, pinned down under a merciless sun for three days with little water? Perhaps someday we'll know.

The shadows had grown long by now, and I turned to follow the last of the visitors to the parking lot. At that moment a yell, free and exultant, came faintly from the battlefield behind me. No one was in sight. A hawk? Perhaps, but the slowly darkening vault of blue sky was empty.

The Little Bighorn Battlefield is a somber place even on a bright summer day. Here hundreds of men died, both Indian and white, and echoes of that tragic struggle linger. Wish their spirits well.

THE INFAMOUS
SHORTY YOUNG

HAVRE BENEATH THE STREETS
100 3rd Avenue
Havre, Montana 59601
406-265-8888

Ghostly Activity Level: Moderate

HISTORY: In 1892, a settlement that had grown up around a railroad siding called Bull Hook was renamed "Havre," in honor of early settlers from France. Due to the town's remote location and proximity to the Canadian border just 30 miles away, Havre soon became one of the roughest towns in the country. In 1904 a devastating fire burned down most of Havre's business district. As soon as the ashes cooled, merchants set up shop in the basements of their buildings. Once rebuilding was complete, most of the basement shops were abandoned, forgotten for decades. In 1989 Frank DeRosa and several other Havre residents decided to clear out the basements and the tunnels connecting the buildings and set up a display of how Havre looked in the old days. In 1994 Havre Beneath the Streets opened. It has become a popular tourist destination, known worldwide.

PHENOMENA: A black bird was seen fluttering in the basement. It disappeared when a tour guide tried to catch it. Voices were heard by an entire tour group when no one else was in the basement. Numerous visitors have commented on a strong "sense of evil" near the brothel and in the office of Havre's most notorious resident, crime boss Shorty Young.

One of Havre's reputedly haunted sites is the historic Park Hotel, built in 1910 and recently renovated. My friend Frank and I both enjoy the ambiance of older hotels, haunted or otherwise. Although we prowled the corridors until almost midnight, all was peaceful, and we finally retired to our comfortable room for a good night's rest.

The next morning we asked the hotel's owner, Kurt Johnson, about the alleged haunting. Johnson told us that he had often worked by himself late at night in the building during the restoration, but never experienced anything unusual. He doesn't discount the possibility of a haunting, however, because the housekeeper once told him that she occasionally heard doors slamming when no one else was around. A long-term resident of the hotel who overheard our conversation volunteered that objects were sometimes moved around in his room during the night. He also suggested that we tour the underground tunnels that once linked buildings in downtown Havre, since he'd heard voices speaking Chinese in the opium den exhibit when no one else was there.

Our ears pricked up at that and we promptly headed over to the Havre Railroad Museum to buy tickets for the tour. The museum was crowded with tourists from all over the world. I could pick out Scandinavian and Dutch languages, and Canadian accents, as well as several I couldn't identify in the conversations around us.

When our young guide appeared, I quietly asked her about ghosts in the tunnels. She'd had no encounters herself, but acknowledged that a number of tourists and at least one of the tour guides, a history teacher at the local high school, had encountered something uncanny on the tour.

She led us to the steps leading down to the tunnels, pointing out opaque-blue glass squares set into the pavement that had once admitted daylight to the walkways below. The first exhibit was the Holland and Son Mercantile, with its antique cash registers, and high shelves lined with canned goods and other merchandise. While the group listened to our guide, I had a sudden urge to look behind us. No one was visible, but I deliberately lingered to take a quick photograph as the group moved on to the next exhibit. A digital photograph revealed a large orb hovering in mid-air just inside the doorway. Was it a flash reflection off a dust mote? It's possible, although our passage through that entry hadn't seemed to stir up any dust.

I caught up with the rest of the group as they left Wright's Dental Office, complete with reclining chair and foot-powered drill. Next was the Sporting Eagle Saloon. The bar was constructed of planks laid across barrels. Bottles, poker chips, and cards were set out on tables. The saloon seemed to have an atmosphere of gaiety and excitement about it, as if the gamblers and drinkers had just stepped out and would return as soon as our tour left.

Next stop was the brothel. Men had used the tunnel system to reach the brothel from nearby hotels without being seen. One partitioned area contained an elaborate bed and a red chair that had belonged to Lt. John "Blackjack" Pershing, who had been stationed at nearby Fort Assinniboine. Later, as General Pershing, he would command U.S. forces in World War I.

The Bruce Clyde Livery Barn and Feed Store had a large display of saddles and other tack. Pioneer Meat Market, farther along the passage, still held the original equipment used for making sausages, along with display cases full of imitation meats. Gourley Brothers Bakery contained the original oven and other baking equipment.

Next was the office of the infamous C. W. "Shorty" Young. Seated before a big rolltop desk was a mannequin in 1920s-era shirt and vest; the head with its slicked-back hair was turned to look at us with what seemed a challenging stare. The figure was extremely lifelike, and in the dim light an air of almost tangible menace seemed to emanate from that silent figure.

Several of us instinctively recoiled at the sight of the mannequin. I had never heard of Shorty Young, but it was obvious that his influence could still be felt here—and it definitely wasn't good.

Our guide explained that although Young had been short in stature at five feet, two inches, he had been a "very big" man during his lifetime. Young was Havre's vice lord, widely involved in prostitution, gambling, and bootlegging. On the surface he was quiet and polite, but at his core was absolutely ruthless. Those who crossed him ended up in the Milk River, or just disappeared.

The rolltop desk in the exhibit had actually belonged to Young, as had the wall safe. The glass doors on the wall and the chandelier were from Young's saloon, the Mint, located directly above the office. Even the letters on the wall were originals signed by Young. Antiques dealers and museum curators have told me that spirits are often drawn to items they used in life. Young's spirit may or may not be present, but his baleful influence still permeates his office, and those who are sensitive enough may feel uneasy in the vicinity.

When I tried to take a photo of the display, my camera's batteries died. I borrowed Frank's camera and snapped two quick shots of the office. Both showed odd streaks, probably caused by the dim light. It was curious, though, especially since my camera worked just fine at the next exhibit, Tamale Jim's Afghani-Mexican eatery.

Boone's Drugstore was stocked with bottles and boxes of old-time medicines. Like many drugstores in the old days, it included a soda fountain and a jukebox.

Wah Sing Laundry offered its customers clean clothes and hot baths, both a definite luxury at the time. Off to one side is a mockup of an opium den, patterned after the three known to have existed in Havre. It contained a bunk bed and a mannequin smoking an opium pipe. This was where Dave, the long-term resident of the Park Hotel, claimed to have heard voices speaking in Chinese. I took a few photos, but nothing unusual showed up.

Our final stop was the Holland Funeral Home, with its antique organ and funeral parlor. Then we followed our guide upstairs to the sunlight, leaving Havre's rowdy past behind.

Ray Bergh, who teaches at Havre High School, has led tours of Havre Beneath the Streets for over ten years. I contacted him to ask whether he'd ever had a creepy experience in the tunnels.

"About four years ago," Bergh told me, "Frank DeRosa and I were doing a walk-through, sprucing things up here and there. We came in through the mercantile and went through to the bordello, and a bird—a black bird—appeared out of nowhere. It fluttered around the chandelier in the bordello, then headed to the east wall and up into the ceiling joists.

"Frank said, 'Hey, why don't you catch that bird and we'll take it outside.' I shone a flashlight up there and there was no bird. The space between the beams does not open up into the ceiling on top. It's a closed space. There was no bird there. I looked at Frank and said, 'It must have come in through the door.' Frank said, 'I didn't see the bird fly in behind us,' then added, 'We're getting out of here and we're leaving *now!*

He grabbed my arm and ran to the door, just white-faced. Frank was scared to death.

"About two weeks after that I was giving an early morning tour. The businesses topside were not open. I brought the people down and we did the auto shop, the mercantile, the bordello, the tack shop, the meat market. We were standing by the butcher's counter and I was talking and someone said, 'Hey, do you hear voices?' We all quieted, and heard the voices. They sounded jovial, coming from behind the wall to the west in the bordello.

"I said, 'It must be another tour behind us. I'll just go back and tell them to hold back, we'll be out of here in a minute or two.' I walked into the bordello and there was nobody there. Nobody was in the saloon, or in the mercantile. I came out and told my tour group, 'Well folks, we've just had something happen.' They told me, 'The voices quit just as you went around the corner, and when you came back around we heard them again for maybe four or five words.'

"I said, 'There's nobody there.' And one gal asked, 'Shall we continue the tour *very* quickly?' We finished the tour and Frank said to me, 'Hey, you're done early!' One person started to tell him what had happened and he said, 'I don't want to hear about it,' and walked out, again white-faced.

"People still frequently hear voices today. I was going down one Sunday morning opening up, turning on lights, and came into the area where we've set up an old whiskey still from Prohibition days. One of the lights was out. I reached up to unscrew the bulb and it was loose. I screwed it back in, but it was dead. I went to our storage area, got a new bulb, and screwed it in. It worked. I finished opening up and went wandering back and the bulb was out again. I reached up and it was loose. I screwed it back in and it turned on. Then for whatever reason I went back into the meat market through

Shorty Young's office. When I came out, the lightbulb was lying on the floor, broken.

"I muttered and grumbled, went back to the supply room, got a dust pan, and swept it up. Then I put a new bulb in and screwed it really tight. Then I thought, 'Wait a minute, I'm the only one down here.' I dumped the fragments, came back out, and the lightbulb was unscrewed again. I screwed it back in and I just said, 'Get thee behind me,' and the lightbulb stayed on for a long, long time. There really *is* something down there."

At that point I told Bergh about my unexpected reaction to the Shorty Young exhibit. He didn't seem surprised. "I've given tours to people who have come through the saloon, the bordello and Shorty's office, and they have said they feel evil, pure evil, in there," he responded. "Shorty rivaled Al Capone. He had people killed. He was kind and generous to kids who needed food or medical treatment, ponying up money to their mothers. He'd say, 'Don't worry about paying me back in cash.' You can put two and two together. Shorty probably worked it out in bed. He was so hated that they would not mention him by name. Shorty was a snake. He paid his taxes, and back then we had the best law enforcement money could buy, if you know what I mean.

"I had one group come through from Canada, a group of sixteen- and seventeen-year-old girls. They felt very nervous in the bordello. Their leader told me, 'I feel the presence in here of something very evil. I feel as if there are hands moving under my dress.' I answered, 'Okay, shall we go on to the next shop?'

"Shorty controlled at least three of the local brothels, perhaps more. He could have been involved in the one in the Underground. He died in 1946, officially from a heart attack but probably from end-stage syphilis. The reason Shorty was divorced twice was probably because he was checking the merchandise. Shorty died alone and miserable, people didn't want to talk to him. One guy said that before he died he'd become totally insane. People still don't talk about him.

"Most of what happens down there is prankish. The bird— that I can't explain."

You'll enjoy visiting the world-famous Havre Beneath the Streets and the Havre Railroad Museum. Perhaps you, too, will sense something odd during the tour. If you'd like a comfortable base for exploring downtown Havre, try the historic Park Hotel, which may have a slight haunting. Just around the corner from the hotel is the Oxford Bar, proudly unchanged since the 1930s. You can get an old-fashioned milkshake there, and several customers have sensed an unseen presence in the men's room. Just don't tell 'em Shorty sent you.

A GHOSTLY
TRIBUTE

GRANDSTREET THEATER
325 North Park Avenue
Helena, Montana 59624
406-442-4270

Ghostly Activity Level: Low

HISTORY: Today's Grandstreet Theater was designed in 1901 by the famous architect C. S. Haire. The brownstone building served as a Unitarian church from 1901 to 1933. Although the building was constructed primarily for worship services, its first minister, the Reverend Leslie Willis Sprague, intended it to be used for meetings, classes, and social events as well. After a devastating earthquake in 1933 damaged the Lewis and Clark Public Library, the church building was donated to the city of Helena for use as the library. In 1976 the library moved to larger quarters and the former church became the Grandstreet Theater.

PHENOMENA: Ghostly footsteps have been reported, lights sometimes turn themselves on or off, props are moved, doors have been heard opening and closing when no one is visible, cold spots are occasionally noted, and those working in the building often have a sense of being watched.

The haunting at Grandstreet Theater has all the elements of a classic ghost story: a beloved individual, an untimely death, and the return of that individual's spirit. In this case, the ghost is presumed to be that of Clara Bicknell Hodgin, who died unexpectedly in 1905. She was the wife of Edwin Stanton Hodgin, one of the early ministers.

When I contacted Tom Cordingley, managing director of the theater, to ask about the haunting, he replied that there had been no ghostly activity for quite a while, but that I was welcome to stop by anyway.

It didn't surprise me that the haunting at the theater had been quiescent recently. Other haunted venues have reported that ghostly activity is often sporadic, with no activity for months or even years, and then suddenly there will be a new flurry of phenomena. I knew that Grandstreet Theater was readying a new production, a play by Eugene O'Neill, and that there would be the inevitable hustle and bustle as crew and cast got ready for opening night. Perhaps Clara Bicknell Hodgin, the ghostly lady reputed to haunt the building, would be drawn by curiosity to watch the preparations.

Tom Cordingley met Frank and me in the lobby. Cordingley has been managing director of the theater for ten years, but his connections go back to his youth. His father often brought him to the theater, and both had great affection for the building. Perhaps that's why the ghostly lady may have chosen to grant Cordingley's father a rare tribute.

I asked Cordingley about any personal ghostly experiences he might have had in the building. At first he could recall none, but then he remarked thoughtfully, "I did have one experience when my dad died. I went down to take care of his business and when I came back I really didn't want to go back to work right away."

When he did return to work, something odd happened just

before a performance was about to begin. The audience was seated and the curtains were about to rise when suddenly all the lights went out. "We had to postpone the show for a few minutes," Cordingley told me. "We were trying to figure out what was wrong, but we didn't find anything. The lights just came back on by themselves a few minutes later. I brought an electrician down the next day but he couldn't find anything wrong either."

"Isn't there an old theater tradition of dimming the lights when someone associated with the theater dies?" I asked. "Maybe that was Clara's way of paying tribute to your father."

Cordingley just smiled. "I think it may have been my dad's way of telling me to get to work!"

Perhaps, but a tribute of that sort to a man who genuinely loved the theater would not be surprising from a woman whose kindness is still remembered a century after her death.

Clara Bicknell Hodgin came to Helena in 1903 with her husband, the Reverend Edwin Stanton Hodgin. Clara, a former teacher in Iowa, enjoyed working with children, and her patience, kindness, and lively sense of humor soon made her a favorite with all who knew her. She was a woman of extraordinary intellect who pushed herself and others to reach their full potential. In January 1905 Clara died suddenly of abdominal cancer. The congregation collected funds for a beautiful Tiffany glass window dedicated to her memory. When the building was given to the city of Helena in 1933 and became a public library, the window was taken down and, for a time, forgotten. In 1976 it was retrieved from storage and reinstalled, its glowing colors still beautiful after a hundred years.

The haunting may first have been noticed while the building was in use as a library. Debra Munn, in her *Big Sky*

Ghosts v.1, mentions a former library employee who claimed to have heard footsteps on a staircase. Since then, many people have experienced a variety of phenomena in the building: footsteps, props mysteriously out of place, lights and other electrical equipment turning themselves on or off.

Does Tom Cordingley believe that Clara's spirit may at times watch the performances? "We assume so," he answered, but repeated that nothing unusual has been seen or heard for several years, ever since the balcony where Clara's presence had frequently been sensed was remodeled. There's a theory that if a haunted building is gutted or remodeled, the emotional energies that have been absorbed by the wood or stone over the years dissipate and the haunting may cease.

I decided to try to find out whether Clara was still present. While Frank stayed below in the auditorium watching the crew get ready for opening night, I climbed the stairs to the balcony.

I hesitated for a moment in the doorway. The balcony was empty, at least to the eye, but it felt *inhabited.* The hair at the back of my neck bristled.

"Clara Bicknell Hodgin," I intoned *a la* television's *Most Haunted* crew, "are you here? Can you make your presence known?" I waited, not knowing what to expect but instinctively certain that a ghostly presence was indeed very close to me.

The seconds ticked past and nothing happened. There were no knocks on the wall, no phantom footsteps, no blast of icy air. Perhaps Clara declined to respond because she was an Edwardian lady and such a dramatic response would not have seemed proper. Or perhaps the sense of presence was all imagination, and there was no one else in the balcony with me.

I intended to take a few photographs of the stagehands

working below, so I wended between the rows of seats to the far side of the balcony. Instead of taking photos of the stage, however, I felt a sudden urgent impulse to take a photo looking back across the balcony to the doorway. After that, I photographed the theater crew setting up props on stage.

That evening, when I looked at the balcony photo I had shot on impulse, I saw a large, intense orb hovering about five feet above the floor just a few seats away from me. Orbs are considered by some to be spirit energy. They have been captured by all types of cameras, eliminating the possibility of a malfunction in one type of camera. Another possibility, of course, is that the "orb" was simply a flash reflection off a dust mote. I'd be more inclined to believe that explanation if I hadn't first sensed a strong presence in the balcony. Perhaps Clara had made her presence known after all.

Another photograph I shot from the balcony showed a second orb, this one hovering near a stagehand's right shoulder as if it were watching the activity with great interest. And indeed, several people who have worked in the building over the past 30 years have reported feeling someone behind and slightly above them, watching whatever they happened to be doing.

Days later, when I finally had time to review the audio recording of my interview with Tom Cordingley, I got another surprise: an unidentified voice on the audiotape. At the point where Cordingley told me how much his father had enjoyed the theater, an elderly male voice on the tape cut in with an enthusiastic "Yeah!"

Does the senior Mr. Cordingley still delight in visiting Grandstreet Theater, or did the ghostly voice belong to someone else? It's difficult to identify a recorded voice from just one spoken word, so perhaps we'll never know. In either case, it appears that Clara Bicknell Hodgin is no longer the only spirit to visit this theater.

Reserve a seat in the balcony when you attend a play at Grandstreet Theater. And if you are lucky enough to glimpse a beautiful lady in old-fashioned clothing seated in the shadows nearby, just nod politely. You'll be sharing the balcony with the spirit of Clara Bicknell Hodgin.

THE CAMAS WATCHMAN

MONTANA HIGHWAY 382
Perma to Hot Springs, Montana

Ghostly Activity Level: Low

HISTORY: State Highway 382 is a two-lane secondary road in northwestern Montana. As late as 1926 the few roads in the area were listed as "trails" or "unimproved" on maps, so relocating and resurfacing the original road probably occurred during the 1930s.

PHENOMENA: The ghost of a man wearing a long black coat has occasionally been seen by motorists along the road. The sightings date back at least 50 years. No one seems to know who he was, although the old-fashioned lanterns he carries are similar to those in use during the first few decades of the 1900s.

Roy Nollkamper of Cut Bank encountered what may have been a ghost in 1994, while he was driving home at night from Spokane. A skeptic, the encounter is still as fresh in his mind today as the night it happened. Here in his own words is the story of the ghost known as the Camas Watchman.

"Driving back to Cut Bank from Spokane can prove to be a long and arduous trip, especially when you get a late start.

Like many folks who make the trip to Spokane, when the weather is good I usually take the shortcut from Elmo to St. Regis. There are two different routes to take, and I decided to travel the Perma to Hot Springs road. Part of the road is sometimes called the Camas cut-across.

"Part of the cut-across winds up a narrow valley, or coulee in 'flatlander' jargon, which has been locally dubbed Markle Hill. Nearly any time of the day you enter the valley, it will be shaded, and seems to be far removed from the terrain you encounter on either end of the valley. There are several old farm and ranch buildings located along the narrow secondary road as it makes its serpentine way up the grade. The hillsides are dotted with very old and gnarled cottonwood and poplar trees. On the opposite side, in certain places, you can see some rock retaining walls along the side of the hill, where the road was previously located. In some places, the construction is almost a work of art, as the walls were built with native rock, stacked and intricately fitted, having held together for over seven decades without the aid of mortar.

"It was October when I was making this particular trip, and it was well into dusk. A fine mist and occasional fog had been the typical weather since leaving St. Regis. As I started up Markle Hill, I could see the shafts of light from my headlight beams cut through the mist as darkness approached.

"Moving up the narrow road, I noticed what appeared to be two small fires not too far ahead of me. The flames in the mist were haloed with orange flickering light as they reflected off the fog. Rounding several more corners, I came upon the objects and they were indeed fires. In fact, they were two old globe-shaped kerosene lamps with an open flame that were used around road construction sites long ago. I slowed to a crawl and noticed that the flames were very distinct and

I could even see the circular wick on the lamps. The fact that this type of lamp was even there was strange to say the least, but they were located dangerously close to the tall grass at the edge of the road. It was obvious that they should cause a fire, but the grass didn't appear to be affected. I started to look for a place along the narrow road to turn around, thinking that I should move the lamps out of the grass.

"As I steered around the next curve, my lights flashed across the narrow valley to the old rock roadway. For just a few seconds, I caught sight of a man sitting on one of the rock retaining walls. His legs were dangling over the side and he was dressed in a long black coat with a tattered hat, dark trousers, and work boots. It was garb you would expect of a construction worker in the twenties or thirties. Beside him was what appeared to be a small copper pail, which I later determined to be a lunch pail. He was calmly sitting there as my lights momentarily flashed over the scene. I could see his head move as if he was watching me as I drove by. Before I could even think about all this, my lights moved past the site.

"Then, thoughts of what in the world a person was doing out there on such a miserable night, and whether it would be safe to stop, flashed through my mind. I couldn't resist, and it was less than a few hundred feet up the road that I found a spot to turn around.

"On the way back down, my headlights were at the wrong angle to see across the valley to determine if the mystery man was still sitting along the old roadway. Even so, I strained my eyes through the darkness to see if he was still watching me, and shivered at the thought. I drove completely past where the lamps were lit just minutes before, but the roadway was now completely dark. Moving back up the hill again I watched for the lamps but they had disappeared—as had the man dressed in black. The spot where he had been sitting was abandoned and all I could see through the darkness and the mist was the rock of the old roadway.

"As with most people who think they have seen something that may not have really been there, I didn't mention my sighting to anyone. I figured that folks would probably look at me like I had seen one of those elusive UFOs or something even stranger.

"About a month later, I couldn't stand it any longer, and I called a friend of mine who is acquainted with the area and also knows most of the local legends. After listening politely to my story, he said that he hadn't heard anything about the specter out in the area of Markle Hill, but that he would check with a friend of his who might know about things 'like that.' He also intimated that perhaps I shouldn't be driving under the influence of whatever it was that I was taking that night. I knew right away that he was the wrong guy to call!

"Several days passed before I got a call from Joe, who works for a company located in Polson. He is very familiar with the area and has traveled the rural roads for many years. His first words as I picked up the phone were, 'I hear that you had a visit from the Camas Watchman.' Apprehensively, I told him that I thought I had seen someone on the roadway, but it wasn't much of a visit as he hadn't come across from the old road to talk, or even stuck around to wave during my several trips up and down the road that night.

"Apparently there have been numerous sightings by locals in the valley for the last fifty to seventy-five years. No one knows exactly who he is, or was, or why he seems to prefer wandering that particular stretch of highway. He had also been seen late one night several years previous, watching when an abandoned bar and restaurant several miles north of Markle Hill burned to the ground. When officials tried to question him about the fire, he had already disappeared. Joe seemed pretty nonchalant about the whole thing, but I'm not too sure I want to travel up that road at night in the near future.

"In a way, the sighting was appropriate since it was just a week before Halloween when I made my trip up Markle Hill. So, next time you take the shortcut between Elmo and St. Regis, be sure to take Highway 382 between Hot Springs and Perma. As you travel up the narrow valley, pay attention, and maybe you too will have an unexpected visitor."

Some ghosts appear to be nothing more than "place memories," a sort of psychic video recording of past events. These ghosts never react to observers. The Camas Watchman, however, turned his head to watch Nollkamper drive past. He seems likely to be an actual spirit, possibly that of one of the men who built the road. Or perhaps Nollkamper himself somehow stepped into the past. If so, the Camas Watchman must have been as startled by his glimpse of a modern automobile as Nollkamper was to see the ghostly antique lanterns at the edge of the road.

THE GHOSTS OF MEADOW BROOK FARM

MEADOW BROOK FARM
100 Meadow Brook Lane
2 miles northeast of Hobson off Highway 200/87 on
 Murray Lane
Hobson, Montana 59452
406-423-5537

Ghostly Activity Level: Moderate

HISTORY: Meadow Brook Farm was established by Thomas R. Murray in 1882. The farmhouse was constructed in 1908, and the large white barn in 1917. It is now owned by the granddaughter of Thomas Murray.

PHENOMENA: The ghost of a young red-haired woman with a 1920s haircut was seen by a member of the Shakespeare in the Parks touring group who were billeted at Meadow Brook Farm. Two guests saw a ghost in the bunkhouse who identified himself as "Sven."

I first heard of a possible haunting at Meadow Brook Farm from Professor Joel Jahnke of Montana State University–Bozeman. Jahnke, artistic director of Shakespeare in the Parks, put me in touch with the student who had encountered a ghost while on tour in 2002.

Susan and Will Dickerson were newlyweds during the summer of 2002. Both had been active in Montana Shakespeare in the Parks for a couple of years. "Will and I were the honeymooning couple," Susan told me, "and organizers in different towns sometimes liked to place us somewhere special. In Hobson, the nicest place for us to stay was what we Shakespeare in the Parkers referred to as the 'haunted bed and breakfast.' I don't know if it has that reputation outside of us, but I think maybe some folks we had toured with before had had some creepy experiences there. I had toured twice before and had avoided staying there because I was afraid of ghosts, but when they told us that they decided the honeymooners should stay there, I didn't want to offend anybody and went along with the idea.

"I did make Will promise to stay awake until I fell asleep, and he kept his promise. I woke up in the middle of the night anyway. I remember I was facing Will when I woke up and was instantly wide awake, and angry with myself for waking up in the first place. I wanted to wake up Will but I decided against it and rolled over on my right side to try to fall back asleep.

"When I did, I saw a woman lying next to me. She was wearing white and had strawberry blonde hair cut in what seemed to be a 1920s style: cropped close at the ears, with straight bangs. She was lying flat with her head resting on her hands.

"She asked me, 'Why are you so afraid of us?'

"At that moment I was both horrified that I was talking to a ghost and embarrassed that she knew I was afraid of her. She seemed just like a normal person who was misunderstood.

"I started to stammer out, 'Oh, it's not you... I don't know...it's just...'

"She interrupted me with 'You know when you're reading a book and...?'

"'Hold on,' I said, and turned over and shook Will awake. When I turned back she was gone.

"So long afterward, I don't really know if it was a dream or if it really happened, but if it was a dream it was one of the most detailed and memorable ones I've ever had. Will also swears that I did shake him awake and told him what happened right there. So maybe it was my subconscious trying to get me to get comfortable with the idea of ghosts, or maybe there's a frustrated 1920s-era ghost out there who had a failed attempt at ghost-human relations. I can't say for sure."

Will Dickerson recalls the event perfectly. "Susan made me promise not to fall asleep before she did. Sometime in the night she rolled over and said, 'Will, wake up!' I did, and was forced to search the room and assure her that it was a dream."

I knew that Frank, Sue, and I would be driving past Hobson the following weekend, en route home from interviewing folks in Fort Benton about their ghosts, so I telephoned Jean Trammell, the owner of Meadow Brook Farm, to tell her about Susan Dickerson's experience with the red-haired ghost and ask whether I might stop by on my way back to Billings.

Trammell agreed, and explained that she lives with her sons in the gray concrete-and-stone farmhouse her grandfather built in 1908. At one time her grandfather had had over 6,000 sheep but, like many other farmers in the 1920s, he lost the farm due to drought. About a dozen families have lived in the house over the years. Trammell bought her grandfather's farm in the 1990s and opened it as a bed and breakfast in 1994. The once-extensive property has shrunk to a more manageable 12 acres these days, mostly leased out. Although none of her guests has ever mentioned a red-haired ghost, Trammell didn't discount the possibility because some of her Scots ancestors had indeed had red hair. Then she added helpfully, "We do have a ghost in the barn though. He was seen by two of my guests."

As we turned off Highway 87 and started up the long farm lane, we were waved down by a man in an approaching car. He turned out to be one of Mrs. Trammell's sons, on his way to town to run an errand. He'd seen us coming and didn't want to miss the chance to tell us his story. He said that he had often heard strange noises while working in the barn. He was accustomed to all the usual creaks and groans of the old building, and these were definitely not caused by wind or the contraction of wood beams.

Jean Trammell met us on the porch and then gave us a tour of her beautiful home. It was filled with the delectable scent of baked ham, and I recalled that the bed and breakfast was known for its hearty farm breakfasts. The six bedrooms upstairs were cozy and decorated with antiques.

On the way downstairs, the tape recorder I had been using to record the interview with Trammell somehow flew out of my hand and bounced all the way down the stairs. When I picked it up, it continued to run but the entire interview had been erased. I'm not sure whether I simply dropped it or whether it had been swept from my hand. I hadn't sensed anything unusual, but perhaps one of the ghosts had objected to our presence. It wasn't the first time a tape recorder had mysteriously fallen from my hand in a haunted building.

Trammell's other son shared a story about a man who had stayed there for three nights and refused to stay again, claiming the house was haunted and that he'd heard noises all night.

A strong cold front was approaching and the wind was

beginning to pick up, so we all hurried to the barn a couple of hundred feet away. Just inside the entrance was a room with a stove and two bunks. It's fitted up comfortably and looks very snug. Two guests once had a remarkable experience there. During the night one of them awakened to see a tall, broad-shouldered man in the doorway. He told her his name was Sven and that he was looking for a grave nearby. Could she help him find the grave? She replied that she was new here and didn't know anything about a grave. He disappeared, and she went back to sleep.

Later that night, the second woman also awoke to see "Sven." He held out a bouquet of flowers to her and they talked for a few minutes, then he disappeared and she went back to sleep. The flowers, unfortunately, also vanished. Neither woman told the other what had happened during the night. Later that day they discovered they had each experienced something unusual, but did not compare details. They decided to tell Trammell about it separately. She brought out an old photo album from her grandfather's day. Each looked at it individually, and both picked out the same tall man in a photo that had been taken of the Norwegians Mrs. Trammell's grandfather had hired to work on the farm. That, each said with certainty, was the man they had seen during the night, the man who had called himself Sven.

The odd thing about it was that Mrs. Trammell knew of no one who had ever died or was buried on the farm. Whose grave had "Sven" been seeking? And even more mysterious, the photo of the hired men has since disappeared.

If you love a peaceful country night in a cozy bunkhouse or in an antiques-filled room, stay at the Meadow Brook Farm. Not only will you enjoy a fresh farm breakfast the next morning, you may encounter the ghost of Sven, or perhaps the spirit *of the red-haired woman who might have been one of Jean Trammell's ancestors. And you may even find out what the ghost meant to say when she began, "You know when you read a book...?"*

WESTWARD HO THE WAGONS!

SOUTH OF INTERSTATE 94
Near Hysham, Montana

Ghostly Activity Level: Low

HISTORY: In May 1864, Jim Bridger led a group of people with Conestoga wagons along what became known as the Bridger Trail, from Fort C. F. Smith to the Montana gold fields of Virginia City. The route was used by nine other wagon trains that year, the last train also led by Bridger.

PHENOMENON: A phantom wagon train was seen in the early 1970s by two long-distance truckers who were driving on Interstate 94, west of Miles City.

The story of the ghostly wagon train was related to me in the 1970s by my long-time friend and mentor, Jack Travis. Jack was of Scots and Cherokee descent, a big man who nevertheless moved as soundlessly as a panther. A born adventurer, he was one of the American volunteers who flew Spitfires with the British during World War II. He was an avid outdoorsman, an amateur archaeologist, and a ghost hunter long before it became fashionable. I had many enjoyable—and sometimes chilling—adventures in the '70s staking out haunted sites with Jack and a group of others interested in the paranormal. We lost touch after I moved to Billings, but I never forgot him. Nor, apparently, did he forget me. Just before bedtime one night I went downstairs to make sure my front door was securely locked. When I turned to go back upstairs, I saw the gray, transparent figure of a man floating at the top of the stairs. The figure had squared shoulders, a short neck, and appeared emaciated, with ribs visible. Something about it seemed familiar, although I couldn't place it at the time. The featureless, cloudy head was turned to the west, but as I stared at it in shock, it slowly rotated and seemed to look directly at me. A moment later the figure glided along my upstairs hallway toward the east. As soon as I could force myself to move, I bounded up the stairs and looked down that hallway. The figure was gone.

I didn't know that Jack had died that night of a massive stroke. He had been ill for a long time and had lost a lot of weight prior to his death. He had had squared shoulders and a short, thick neck. I'll always believe that his spirit looked in on me that night.

The story that follows is exactly as Jack told it to me. Only the names of the drivers have been altered for the sake of privacy.

Steve B. was relaxed, his hands resting lightly on the wheel. The big diesel was purring along, the trailer steady behind him. He glanced at the tachometer. The dial was hanging right where it was supposed to be as the big truck pounded steadily westward on I-94. Steve was about two hours out of Miles City, Montana, where they had refueled and changed drivers.

Herb D., his relief driver, was resting quietly in the sleeper in the back of the cab and probably wouldn't awaken until they stopped in Billings for breakfast. The headlights were creating puddles of yellow incandescence through the pre-dawn hush of an August morning.

Glancing out the cab window, Steve could see in the rear-view mirror the shimmering side of the trailer and the empty highway unwinding behind him, stretching to the horizon where the eastern sky was just beginning to lighten.

He switched his attention back to the road in front of him. Suddenly he frowned. He thought he'd glimpsed something to the left of the highway, about a quarter mile to the south. It was a flickering reddish light, almost like a smoldering grass fire.

By downshifting and judicious use of his air brakes, he slowed the big rig to a crawl and surveyed the scene. To his surprise, the firelight suddenly went out, as if someone had extinguished it. Then he saw something else, something that raised the hair on his arms. A huge circle of Conestoga wagons, the prairie schooners of a bygone era, was unraveling like some huge snake, the horses throwing themselves into their collars at the shrill urging of their drivers.

Unable to believe his eyes, Steve brought the rig to a complete stop and reached back into the sleeper to awaken Herb. His partner crawled sleepily out of the bunk and into the cab of the truck. "What's up?" he yawned. "Billings already?"

Steve pointed silently.

"Gotta be a movie outfit," Herb said at last. But there were no supply trucks, no cameras, and, most important at that hour, no floodlights. They rolled down the windows of the cab so they could see better. The wagon train gradually straightened out and headed westward as they watched, both of them wide awake now, the scouts in the lead and outriders flanking the train on both sides.

One of the outriders, a burly man with long hair and a full beard, rode within 100 yards of the highway where the big truck sat, its diesel engine rumbling and red and yellow clearance lights outlining the trailer. The rider was carrying a Civil

War-vintage lever-action carbine across his saddlebow and he looked through the trailer as if it weren't there, as though he saw nothing but empty prairie.

Just then the two truckers noticed that the grayness in the east had given way to the rosy glow of dawn. As daylight increased, the wagons began to shimmer into invisibility. In less than two minutes, Steve and Herb could see nothing on the prairie but scrub grass and sunlight.

Steve put the rig into gear and they started rolling again, each man busy with his own thoughts. There was a sort of tacit agreement between them that neither would mention their bizarre early morning experience to other truckers, for they knew they would be ridiculed all the way to the West Coast if the story got out.

Long afterward, Jack told me, "The only reason the drivers broke their silence was that Steve knew me and trusted me not to make a laughingstock of either driver. Both also wanted some answers. Neither was a very religious man, and both were intelligent enough to have a burning curiosity about the phenomenon. I'm afraid I was able to help them very little. I did point out the possibilities: they might have been hallucinating, a supposition they both hotly denied; that the particular stretch of I-94 paralleled an old wagon trail and that for a short time the truckers had stepped into the past; that it actually was a movie company on location, a possibility we were able to rule out completely; that a wagon train had been ambushed on that spot and all its people massacred. However, a search of newspaper archives revealed no account of a wagon train being attacked along the Yellowstone River, nor at any other spot between Miles City and Billings.

"I am convinced the two men saw what they so vividly described to me, but I have no convincing explanation. Perhaps someone, someday, will manage to trace the story of the ghostly wagon train that vanishes when the sun rises."

Did the two truckers glimpse of one of the ten wagon trains that traveled the Bridger Trail in 1864? The description of the wagons and weaponry fits the time frame, though Bridger's Trail is thought to have been slightly farther west. Wagons did stray from established routes depending on changing conditions, and the rutted remains of many old wagon trails still crisscross the prairie south of the Yellowstone. Perhaps the ghostly wagon train will again appear to another fortunate traveler who just happens to be in the right place at dawn on an August morning.

CONRAD MANSION
MUSEUM

CONRAD MANSION NATIONAL HISTORIC SITE
330 Woodland Avenue
Kalispell, Montana 59901
406-755-2166

Ghostly Activity Level: Moderate

HISTORY: Charles Conrad, one of the founders of the city of Kalispell, grew up on his family's plantation in Virginia. After the Civil War, Charles returned home to find that the plantation could no longer support him in the elegant Southern style in which he had been raised, so he and his brother William headed west to make their fortunes. Within a few years they owned a thriving freight business in Fort Benton. In 1891, Charles moved to the Flathead Valley, platted the city of Kalispell, and continued his involvement in the livestock industry, real estate, banking, and mining.

In 1881, Conrad married Alicia "Lettie" Davenport Stanford. They had three children, Charles D., Catherine, and Alicia Ann. Conrad died in 1902 at age 52. After his death, Alicia Ann became her mother's companion. After Lettie's death in 1923, Alicia Ann married in 1924 and again in 1927. She gave the house and most of its original furnishings to the city of Kalispell in 1974. The house opened as a museum in 1975. Alicia Ann Conrad Campbell died in 1981, age 88.

PHENOMENA: A staff member has repeatedly thought she saw someone moving in the master bedroom while she was in the Great Hall. No one was on the second floor at the time. A visitor sensed a little girl in the master bedroom, and people walking past outside have seen a little girl looking out from the upper windows. The smell of burned toast has been noticed in the empty kitchen and the faint scent of cigar smoke in the master bedroom.

The Conrad Mansion was not yet open when we drove up, but several tourists were already waiting by the entrance. The property covers three acres, including the site of former stables across the street, and the mansion itself is set regally amidst lovingly restored gardens. The sky was darkly overcast that morning and the salvia glowed a deep crimson in the subdued light. Hummingbirds darted from flower to flower, and I described the scene into my tape recorder while my friends Frank and Sue took photos of the house. I've learned over the years that it's much easier to record details and interviews than to try to decipher my scribbles later. When I pushed the "play" button to make certain the recorder was working properly, however, I discovered that the tape was blank. The fast forward, reverse, and play functions worked perfectly, but the record function was not working. I tried the backup tape recorder with the same results. Neither would record in the vicinity of the mansion. It's not unusual to have cameras and tape recorders malfunction in haunted premises, but for both to fail at the same time when they had been working perfectly the day before *was* unusual—and intriguing.

Promptly at ten o'clock the doors opened and we followed the other tourists into the baronial Great Hall. A young woman wearing a Victorian gown greeted us and provided a brief history of the house before beginning the tour. The 13,000-square-foot, 26-room home had taken three years to build. Thanks to the foresight of Alicia Conrad Campbell, 90 percent of the furnishings were original, making the house a time capsule of elegant life in the early twentieth century.

Many great houses of that era have massive stone fireplaces, Tiffany-style stained glass, and oak paneling, but the Conrad mansion has those and more: a freight elevator, dumbwaiter, built-in fire hoses at each level, an intercom, and drinking fountains.

We followed our guide through various rooms on the main level, then up the stairs to the second floor. Anyone standing near the railing that ran the length of the second-floor corridor could easily see—and be seen by—people in the Great Hall below. I recalled what a staff member had told me previously. She had been standing in the Great Hall when she glimpsed a figure moving in the Master Bedroom. No one had been on the second floor at the time.

Several other bedrooms are on the second floor. In one of them, the Gray Room, I caught a whiff of an elusive fragrance quite distinct from the odor of the flowers in a nearby vase. The fragrance was quite light and delicate, and soon faded away.

The master bedroom, with its canopied bed, had been the scene of sad events. Both Charles Conrad and his wife Lettie had died there, Conrad in 1902 and Lettie in 1923. I lingered behind the group to take a photo, and for a moment detected the faint scent of cigar or pipe tobacco. It was so fleeting that I couldn't be certain which it was, or if I had smelled anything at all.

"Did Mr. Conrad smoke a cigar or a pipe?" I later asked Kate Daniels, the mansion's director.

"He smoked a pipe," she replied. I explained what I thought I had smelled, and that phantom odors are probably the most common type of haunting. If I really had smelled tobacco, I added, the little girl who had been seen several times might not be the only family member to occasionally return in spirit to the mansion.

Conrad's presence seemed even more likely when we visited what he called his "Sky Office" on the third floor. Conrad used the room when he wanted peace and quiet, particularly when his health began to deteriorate. When I poked my head inside the doorway it felt obvious that the room was occupied, although I could see no one. The conviction that someone unseen was present was so strong that I backed out of the room, feeling as if I should apologize for the intrusion. When I came back to the room a few minutes later, the sense of presence was gone from the empty room.

A small room crammed with antique dolls may also be a focus for paranormal activity. A staff member told me she had taken a tour group up to the third floor once and a little boy adamantly refused to go into the doll room. He told his father he could see a little girl playing there. None of the adults could see anything unusual.

According to another staff member, a neighborhood couple went up the fire escape one day to peer into the house. They claimed that they saw a little girl riding a tricycle across the bare boards of the third floor. On another occasion, a chaperone for an Upward Bound group came to the docent after touring the house and told her that there was a little girl in the master bedroom who was very lonely. He sensed her, but did not see her.

Who is the little girl? She may be Alicia Ann, the youngest of the Conrad children. Her brother and sister were much older and away at school for most of each year, so Alicia's childhood must have been relatively lonely. Thirteen cats and a horse provided companionship, and perhaps the house itself, with its doll room and an attic perfect for roller-skating, came to be a substitute of sorts for a human playmate. Certainly the house meant a great deal to Alicia Ann, both as a child and as a grown woman.

One of the most interesting sightings occurred a few years ago when the roof was being repaired. A roofer happened to glance down at a window and saw a young girl standing inside, watching him. If she was indeed the spirit of Alicia Ann, perhaps the roof repair had triggered memories of a dreadful night in late October 1910, when the mansion was almost destroyed by fire. While her mother called the fire department, 18-year-old Alicia Ann grabbed the fire hose on the second floor and dragged it out onto the roof, where she could direct the stream of water onto the fire. Her efforts held the fire in check until the fire department arrived, but the mansion was heavily damaged.

There are other indications that life goes on unseen in the mansion: one of the staff was cleaning on the third floor when she heard whispering. It was definitely the sound of a human voice, but as is usual with an audible haunting, the words could not be made out. A volunteer has occasionally noticed the unmistakable odor of burnt toast in the empty kitchen first thing in the morning. And at times someone—or something—objects to the use of the vacuum in the master bedroom. One day the assistant director was vacuuming in that room. The atmosphere became decidedly uncomfortable, and he found that he was no longer able to push the vacuum forward. He took the hint and retreated.

Perhaps Conrad's wife, Lettie, was responsible for that. The figure of a woman has been seen in a window by a couple driving past. They had known Lettie well during her lifetime, and were certain they were not mistaken.

The Conrad Mansion is one of the most beautiful houses of its era that I have ever visited. Moreover, it has an air of expectancy, as if the family has just stepped into the next room and will return momentarily. That impression is so strong that I could not help but cast a quick look behind me as we passed a long horsehair sofa in a second-floor corridor. For a moment it seemed that someone was seated there, graciously welcoming us to her home.

I gave the unseen presence a nod of thanks—just in case.

The Conrad Mansion is lovely at any time of year, but the gardens are spectacular in late summer. While you're enjoying the flowers, glance up at the third-floor windows from time to time. If you're very lucky, you may catch sight of a little girl smiling back at you. As Director Kate Daniels says, "The Conrad family loved their life in this house and it is impossible not to sense this when you are working in or visiting their home."

GHOSTLY GIGGLES
IN THE NIGHT

THE HISTORIC HOTEL LINCOLN
101 Sleepy Hollow Lane
Lincoln, Montana 59639
406-362-4906

Ghostly Activity Level: Moderate

HISTORY: The bustling placer-mining camp of Lincoln was born in the 1860s, when gold was discovered in nearby Lincoln Gulch. When the gold played out, the town moved to its present location about three miles from the original townsite. The first building erected in the new town was a single-story log hotel called the Halfway House Hotel, which eventually became a boardinghouse for tourists. Leonard Lambkin purchased the hotel in 1918. It was one of artist Charles M. Russell's favorite places, and his signature is preserved on a page from the old hotel register. In 1928, the old hotel either burned down or was moved elsewhere and a new, two-story hotel took its place. Over the years the building was remodeled and bathrooms added to each room. The town of Lincoln is now a resort area with several excellent restaurants and a flourishing artistic community.

PHENOMENA: The strong scent of perfume is sometimes noted in Room 17 of the Hotel Lincoln. Local residents driving past saw the figure of a woman standing in the window at the end of the second-floor corridor. Lights turn themselves on and off, and staff and guests heard the happy giggles of children on the second floor.

"It's gorgeous!" I exclaimed as we turned into the parking lot of the historic Hotel Lincoln. The hotel is indeed impressive, a two-story log building set among tall, graceful ponderosa pines. According to its owners Frank and Cindy Knowles, it also is haunted. While the hotel's address on Sleepy Hollow Lane may conjure up a vision of Washington Irving's Headless Horseman, the ghosts of the Hotel Lincoln are far gentler than Ichabod Crane's nemesis.

The current hotel stands on the site of an earlier hotel built in the mid-1860s. Local residents disagree about what happened to the first hotel. Either the aging building burned to the ground in 1927, or it was dismantled and moved elsewhere. Whatever the building's actual fate, the ghost is locally thought to be that of a prostitute who may have burned to death in the old building, or perhaps simply died in her room during the mining boom of the 1860s. The origin of the ghost may never be determined with any certainty, but too many people have experienced odd phenomena at the hotel over at least the past several decades to doubt that it is haunted.

Labor Day had just passed, and most of the summer visitors had left when Frank and I arrived, so we had been able to book the most haunted room, Number 17, for the night. Frank Knowles met us in the bar. He and his wife Cindy, and sons Brandon and Cole, own the hotel. "You'll be the only guests tonight," he told us matter-of-factly, and handed us his set of master keys. "You can investigate all the rooms if you want to."

My ghost hunter's antennae were already twitching eagerly at the thought of being turned loose in a haunted hotel with permission to roam all over. I wasn't worried that my friend Frank and I would be the sole occupants—living, that is—in the building. After all, the ghosts were reported to be friendly, not about to frighten anyone. Another guest did arrive later that evening, but that didn't affect our anticipation of an enjoyably spooky experience.

We went upstairs to the second floor. Our room was at the very end of a long corridor of polished wood. The boards creaked loudly with every step. This was where previous guests had heard giggling children run up and down the corridor very early in the morning. I paused to look out the window at the end of the corridor, as the ghost is said to have done many times, and then unlocked Room 17.

In the mid-1990s a master craftsman had redone all the woodwork in the hotel. Our room was beautifully paneled, and comfortably furnished with handmade pine furniture. It also was overpoweringly full of a spicy scent I couldn't quite recognize. At first I thought it was a type of potpourri, but there was none in the room. Then I began to wonder if it was a lavender-based perfume, perhaps mixed with other scents as had been the custom in Victorian times. It certainly didn't seem to be a modern perfume, and Knowles had told us that no guest had stayed in the room for the past two days.

The fragrance was real enough; even Frank could smell it, and he has always claimed he has almost no sense of smell. The fragrance was limited to Room 17, as I quickly discovered when I used the master keys to explore the other rooms. All were furnished with beautiful handcrafted furniture and looked very comfortable. I sensed nothing unusual in any of them except Room 21, where my hair stood on end as soon as I entered. This was one of the rooms in which lights sometimes turn themselves on or off when the rooms are unoccupied. In addition, a honeymooning couple had had a strange experience in this room.

"A young couple got married and came to stay in that room," Frank Knowles had told us. "They had brought maybe four or five candles for a romantic evening in there. They came back down to have a drink at the bar and when they went back and unlocked the door, their candles were missing. They were never found."

Maybe the ghostly woman had enjoyed a romantic evening of her own.

"I don't tell people about the stories," Knowles had gone on to say. "But sometimes they walk into that room and their hair stands on end. One guest even came down and asked for a different room. It's just ghostly pranks, though."

When dusk settled over the hotel, we were ready for supper. The restaurant at the Hotel Lincoln is reported to be superb, but unfortunately wasn't open that evening. Frank Knowles suggested that we go to PondeRosa's just a couple of blocks away. First, though, I walked around the outside of the hotel, checking upper-floor windows for unexplained lights or ghostly figures. I saw nothing out of the ordinary, so we left and had an excellent meal.

Knowles had mentioned that guests sometimes reported hearing children running, giggling, along the upstairs corridor at about one or two in the morning, so when we returned to the hotel I set up one of my tape recorders just outside the door of our room. It would turn on only if triggered by a noise, so the tape would last all night unless the ghosts chose to make a long appearance.

Disappointingly, the tape recorder picked up no unexplained noises during the night. One rather odd thing did happen, however. We had left both windows open while we were out to supper, and when we returned the mysterious perfume had faded to the point where it was barely detectable. When I awoke sometime during the night, the fragrance had intensified, even though the windows were still open. The scent seemed to be concentrated right next to the bed. I could see nothing unusual, but couldn't help but wonder whether the ghostly lady had decided to drop by to greet us.

The next morning we met Cindy Knowles, who shared some of her experiences at the hotel. "It was late one night after the restaurant had closed," she began. "Everything down here was dark. My husband, the chef, and I were the only people in the building. There were no guests in the hotel that night. It was winter, and it was cold out. We were sitting at the bar having a beer. Everything else down here was dark: the restaurant, the kitchen, and the back room area where the bathrooms and the gift shop are.

"We were going out to meet somebody, and I decided to use the bathroom first. I went through the darkness to the bathroom. As I was washing my hands, I heard a woman talking, having a conversation with somebody. I didn't know who she was talking to, but she sounded happy. I couldn't make out the words, and I remember thinking that if I were a couple of feet closer I could make out what she was saying.

"At first I thought it was our chef, because he's been known to do funny voices, and it sounded like he and my husband were waiting for me just outside the bathroom. I thought that he was doing a really good voice, because it really sounded like a woman.

"Well, I turned off the bathroom light and opened the door, and the talking cut off. I went around the corner expecting to find the chef and my husband standing there but nobody was there. I came all the way back through the dark restaurant, and I had goosebumps. I asked Frank and the chef if either of them had moved, and they told me they'd stayed in the bar the whole time I was in the bathroom. I told them what I had heard and they just laughed at me.

"The following day I got a call from the previous owner, asking about some paperwork, and I told her my experience. She said, 'Oh, you had an encounter with *her!*'

"The haunting goes back several owners at least. There's a lady who used to work here about four owners ago. She stayed in Room 7, right below Room 17. She said she couldn't even spend the night in there because a glittery light-thing came through the wall and went around her bed. She just jumped up and took off and wouldn't stay here again.

"One night, we had guests staying in Room 3, and the lady said to me in the morning, 'You know the guests who are staying above us? Their children are really noisy. They kept running up and down the hall laughing all night.'

"I just looked at her, because nobody was upstairs, and the lights were off. We both went up to look, and sure enough, the hallway was dark and the rooms empty. She said, 'Okay, now I have goose bumps!'

"Our chef has Room 10 now, and he said about one or two o'clock one night he heard my kids running up and down the upstairs hallway. I told him my kids had been in bed at our house since nine o'clock. He knew there were no guests in the hotel that night, so that's why he thought it was my kids.

"It happens more in winter, maybe every few months. Once the people in Room 7 heard noises from Room 17, right above them. It sounded like someone scraping luggage across the floor. There was no one up there that night, either."

I asked Cindy about the strong scent in our room. She had never smelled anything like it before, and told us that no guest had been in the room for the previous two days. She said that the housekeeper had noticed it on several occasions, however, always in Room 17. It happened rarely, and at long intervals. No explanation for the scent has been found.

We drove away from the historic Hotel Lincoln with a promise to come back for a visit on a cold, quiet, winter night, when ghostly activity tends to pick up. Perhaps we will be fortunate enough to hear the giggles of little ghosts running in the upper hallway. For them, playtime never ends.

Guests at the Hotel Lincoln will enjoy gourmet meals in its fine restaurant and a comfortable stay in one of its 14 rooms. As an added bonus, there's the chance of an encounter with the ghostly woman who sometimes looks out the window at the end of the second-floor corridor, or perhaps hearing the echoes of childish laughter from the past.

THE NIGHT THE CEILING CRASHED DOWN

CLUB 519
519 Main Street
Miles City, Montana 59301
406-232-5133

Ghostly Activity Level: Moderate

HISTORY: The First National Bank, designed by well-known architect C. S. Haire, was built in 1910. For many years the second floor hosted the prestigious Miles City Club, Montana's oldest social club, founded in 1884. Some of its illustrious guests included Theodore Roosevelt, the Marquis de Mores, and Pierre Wibaux. The formerly private club is now a fine public restaurant.

PHENOMENA: A blurry figure was seen on the stairway that leads up to the restaurant. Cold spots and odd noises were noticed by bartenders when closing up for the night. An enormous crash as if the entire ceiling had caved in was heard by one of the bartenders as she locked the stairway gate one evening.

There's no mistaking the fact that the building that now houses Club 519 was once a bank, with impressive stone columns, oversized windows, and classical facade. The restaurant is on the second floor, reached by a long flight of stairs.

Currie Colvin, manager of the haunted Montana Bar, suggested the restaurant when I asked him to recommend a good place to have supper. He mentioned nothing about a haunting at Club 519, and I had no reason to suspect that the club's dinner guests might occasionally have a brush with the uncanny.

The moment Frank, Sue, and I started up the stairs to the restaurant, however, Sue turned to me and said meaningfully, "I have a headache. I think there's a ghost here."

Many people experience a physical reaction to the presence of ghosts. It may be a headache like Sue's, or a feeling of tightness in the chest, or perhaps the sensation that the hairs at the back of one's neck are stirring. In my case, it's a sense of heavy pressure, as if I'm at the bottom of a swimming pool. Over the years, Sue and I have learned to trust what we call our "alarm bells."

There was nothing in the least spooky about the restaurant itself. Most of the tables were occupied so the servers were busy. Dinner was excellent, but for some reason my gaze was continually drawn to the tall windows. I had a strong impression that a woman had often sat at the window in the distant past, absently stroking a cat while gazing over the streets. There was a pleasant, somehow companionable feeling about it, as if the woman had made her home here.

We decided to wait until after dessert to ask about ghosts. By then the crowd had thinned and our hostess, Ramona Christianson, was able to take a short break.

Christianson told us that she had worked as head waitress at Club 519 for six years. Before that, she was in charge of hiring at the Olive Hotel, where we were staying that night.

As we had suspected, Club 519 was indeed haunted. "There are two ghosts, one male and the other female," Christianson said. "The male ghost doesn't like it when it gets busy in here, or when there are big parties. He likes it quiet. When there are parties going on, bottles tend to fall off the shelves, the waitresses can't carry their food, things fall off our trays. It's really bizarre.

"Generally we just see a grayish blur and the room will get really cold. I'm not familiar enough with the history of this building to determine who it is, and we can't make out the style of clothes well enough to date him."

Bartender Kim Smith took advantage of a lull at the bar to tell us about her experience. Smith has worked at Club 519 for five years. Twice she saw the ghost of a woman, both times on the landing, as if she had just come up the stairs and was about to turn the corner to enter the restaurant. The ghost appeared slightly built and was wearing a "Little House on the Prairie"-style dress.

"Her face looked blurred," she said. "I couldn't make out her features."

Late one night, Smith had an alarming experience that left her puzzled. Everyone had gone home, so she closed the restaurant as usual and started down the stairs to the ground floor. Halfway down she paused to lower the wrought-iron gate that blocks the stairway. Just as she locked the gate she heard a tremendous crash from the restaurant above.

"It sounded like the whole ceiling came down," she recalled. Reacting instinctively, she ran down the stairs, snapped off the lights, and ran out the door. The next day, when she came to work she expected to find repair crews replacing a damaged ceiling, but only the usual employees were on duty in the restaurant and nothing appeared to be out of place at all.

"I asked if they had found anything on the floor when they opened that day," she said, "but they hadn't. I told them what had happened. We couldn't figure out what had caused the noise."

There's no legend to account for the haunting, but there's no doubt the restaurant is haunted. Other bartenders have encountered the ghosts of Club 519, felt cold spots, seen a blurred figure on the landing, and heard odd noises, always late at night after customers have left.

The haunting may be associated with whatever was on the site before. "The female ghost looks like she's from the homesteader era," Smith said. "She doesn't wear a bonnet, and her hair is scraped back."

While Smith was speaking we were all suddenly engulfed by intense cold. We looked around to see if we were sitting under an air-conditioning vent. The nearest one was about ten feet away and obviously not the source of the abnormal cold that seemed to hover above our table. On impulse I stood up and took a photo with my digital camera. The photo showed an orb hovering near the ceiling about 15 feet beyond the air-conditioning vent. At the same time, the tape recorder I had been using to record the interview recorded a strange whispering voice that did not belong to any of us. It sounded like a woman's voice, commenting on our discussion. Unfortunately, her words overlapped Kim Smith's and only two words could be made out: "No" and, after a few indecipherable words, "....return."

I suddenly remembered the woman I had sensed sitting beside the window looking out over the town. "Was the building ever divided into apartments?" I asked. Smith didn't think so, but perhaps research into the building's 1930s and 1940s history would provide an answer. Without historical input, it's hard to know who the ghost or ghosts may have been. The woman in the "Little House on the Prairie" dress may have homesteaded in that era, while the man who dislikes big parties may have been a member of the Miles City Club, someone who enjoyed the peace and quiet of an exclusive gentlemen's club and resents the intrusion by large groups of people. As for the lady I sensed who may once have sat beside the window, stroking her cat, perhaps she lived in an apartment or worked in an office on the second floor.

Whoever the ghosts were or are, the employees at Club 519 take them in stride. After all, even though ghosts don't leave tips, they do add a bit of spice to a day's work.

Be sure to try the huckleberry ice cream if you stop in to eat at Club 519. And if the space around your table suddenly turns abnormally cold, you may have been joined by one of the club's unseen visitors.

OLIVE'S ROOM

OLIVE HOTEL
501 Main Street
Miles City, Montana 59301
406-234-2450

Ghostly Activity Level: Moderate

HISTORY: The Olive Hotel was built in 1898 on the site of a saloon reputedly owned by General George A. Custer's horse wrangler, Charlie Brown. Originally known as the Leighton Hotel, the building was listed in the National Register of Historic Places in 1988. In 1908 the architect Grover C. Pruett redesigned the front of the Renaissance Revival-style hotel. Census records show that the Kennie family owned and lived in the hotel in 1910. One of the daughters, Olive Kennie Gifford, is reputed to haunt Room 250. She died in 1971.

PHENOMENA: Staff have reported the materialization of a female ghost thought to be Olive Kennie, daughter of a former owner. Guests in "Olive's Room" have noted a toilet tank chain that swings by itself and an indentation that suddenly appears on the bedspread even though no one is visible.

Frank, Sue, and I had made reservations at the historic Olive Hotel simply because we enjoy the ambiance of older buildings. We hadn't expected to find a haunting thrown in free of charge.

The Olive is conveniently located in downtown Miles City. Built in 1898, it was an upscale hotel featuring a lobby with a marble floor, Tiffany-style colored glass above each window, and heavy oak doors. The hotel quickly became a social center for area ranchers and travelers. As the years passed and motels were built at the edge of the city, the Olive's fortunes declined, and at one point the third floor was used to house senior citizens with modest incomes.

The present owners have worked hard to update the hotel. It's still a work in progress, but the accommodations are clean and comfortable. The restaurant on the main floor serves enormous omelets that could keep even a hardworking rancher fueled for hours. Prices are modest and if you want to stay there, reserve your room early—the hotel is often fully booked, especially during the annual Bucking Horse Sale on the third weekend of May.

After the three of us dropped our luggage in our rooms, we went back down to ask the desk clerk if the hotel happened to be haunted. He had heard that Room 250 was haunted by someone named Gus, but couldn't recall more details.

Owner Carol Schneider was able to clarify the story. The Olive was definitely haunted, she told me, but the ghost wasn't Gus. Gus was a fictional character from the television miniseries *Return to Lonesome Dove* who had suffered a dramatic death in front of the cameras in Room 250. Somehow he had become confused with an actual ghost whose family had once lived in the hotel.

Schneider, who managed the hotel for three years before she and her partners bought it, was quite open about the haunting. "I didn't believe in ghosts at first," she told us. "Then I had an experience in Room 250, Olive's room."

Room 250 is referred to as the Antique Room. It has a beautiful old cabinet radio from the late 1920s or 1930s, a brass bedstead, an antique dresser, and a photo of Olive on the wall above the bed. The bathroom has a pull-chain toilet and a huge claw-foot bathtub on a marble floor.

"A couple of times guests have left suddenly," Schneider said. "They said the water turned itself on and the toilet flushed itself. It's not just the plumbing. I took a prospective buyer and his wife around once, and when we got to that room, the toilet flushed and we all saw the toilet tank chain start to swing. The buyer and his wife left and never came back."

Ramona Christianson, who now works at the haunted Club 519 not far from the hotel, also had some odd experiences at the hotel when she worked there from 1994 to 2000. Christianson and her partner, James, had heard stories that the hotel was haunted, but never believed it.

"When the hotel turned one hundred in 1998 we did a bunch of research on it," Christianson told me. "We looked up everything there was on it. Meanwhile I had decorated the place with great big pictures. One was called 'Dining at the Ritz.' The picture hung in the dining room of the hotel. To the public, it looked like a group of people sitting on a terrace. My partner and I spent many hours there after hours, and the picture would change. A man in a long white beard would appear in a corner of the painting, then there was a girl, and in the center was a man with a dark beard. Lights would twinkle and the girl would turn. She really loved parties. We'd sit and talk to her and ask her things like, 'Should we have prime rib for Mother's Day?' and the lights would get really bright. 'Should we have ham for a side dish?' No reply. So we knew that was a no-no. I still have that painting. To this day it can't come out of the closet because weird things will happen at my home.

"That wasn't the only weird thing that happened when I was at the hotel. Olive married a man named James. My partner's name was James so Olive was very protective of him, too. Late at night, after we'd had big banquets in the dining room, we'd be counting our money and we'd see her in one of the booths. You could make out her long skirt and a high-collared mutton-sleeved dress, but she didn't look particularly solid. Her hair was pulled back in a tight bun.

"The whole Kennie family lived in the hotel around 1910. Olive's room used to be toward the front of the building, not Room 250. Later, her things were moved to 250, which was called the Antique Room. When I was there, some remodeling was being done, and the workers took out Olive's wardrobe, the iron bed, and her washstand. When they came back the next day everything was back in place. It freaked out the janitor. He locked the door of the room and wouldn't go back.

"One day I was standing in the bathroom of Room 250 with Jim, and it was absolutely quiet. There's no vent in there, but the bath curtain moved in and out by itself. I grabbed Jim's hand, and the toilet flushed. When we walked out of the bathroom into the room, there was an indent on the bedspread, just like someone had been sitting there."

After hearing those stories, I knew I had to see Room 250. Unfortunately it was already occupied by the time we got back from dinner. The next morning I waited until the guests in Olive's room had checked out, and then asked permission to view the room. Carol Schneider happened to be on duty at the front desk and promptly handed me the old-fashioned key.

We unlocked the door and cautiously peered inside, not sure what to expect. The room had not been made up, but other than rumpled bedclothes everything looked perfectly normal. Reassured, we stepped inside, and were immediately surrounded by one of the most intense electrical fields I have ever encountered in a haunted location. If ghosts are a form of electromagnetic energy, as hypothesized, then whatever haunted Olive's room was certainly making its presence known!

We took several photos and then went into the bathroom where Schneider and her prospective buyers had watched the toilet chain swing. Nothing happened. No plunging temperatures, no sense of presence, no self-flushing toilet, no ghostly moans or groans, just tingling skin, and hair that was trying its best to stand on end. I spoke aloud to the ghost, coaxing her to answer some questions in hopes that my tape recorder might pick up a ghostly voice, but nothing unusual was on the tape when I played it back. Sue's camera did capture an intense pink orb, or energy ball, hovering near Olive's wardrobe.

Just in case "Olive" really was present, we thanked her courteously before locking the door and returning the key. Some day we'll return. I have a feeling that a night in Room 250 could prove very interesting indeed!

Call well ahead if you want to reserve Olive's room. It's beautifully decorated with antiques and is usually booked. If you happen to notice an indentation on the bedspread when you enter, don't worry, your invisible roommate doesn't take up much space.

THE 25TH INFANTRY BICYCLE CORPS GHOST

FORT MISSOULA
Missoula, Montana 59804
406-728-3476

Ghostly Activity Level: Low

HISTORY: Fort Missoula was established in 1877 to protect settlers from Indian attacks. Unlike most eastern forts, Fort Missoula had no walls. In 1888, the 25th Infantry, made up of black soldiers, arrived at the fort. In 1896, Lt. James Moss, one of the 25th Infantry's white officers, organized the Bicycle Corps to test the potential of bicycles for military transport. Although the Bicycle Corps made a 1,000-mile trip from Fort Missoula to St. Louis, Missouri in 1897, the Army decided that bicycles were not an efficient means of transportation. The fort later was used to train mechanics during World War I and served as headquarters for the Civilian Conservation Corps during the Depression of the 1930s. During World War II, the fort was used as an alien detention center. Over 1,200 Italians were interned at the fort until they were released in 1944. Over 650 Japanese-American men were also held at the fort before being transferred to other internment camps. The fort was decommissioned in 1947, and many of the buildings demolished or removed from the site. The Army and Navy now have training facilities at the site, and other government agencies lease some of the buildings.

PHENOMENA: Security alarms sometimes go off for no apparent reason. Footsteps were repeatedly heard in the basement of the Quartermaster's Warehouse when no one was there. Objects are mysteriously moved around. A staff member was touched by a cold invisible hand. Martial music played after closing when no one was there. A former curator saw a "military-looking" ghost.

Darla Bruner is no stranger to ghostly phenomena. For about 18 months she was Director of Education for the haunted Western Heritage Center in Billings, and occasionally heard ghostly footsteps outside her office there when she was working late. At first she assumed that one of her coworkers had come in. "Kevin? Al?" she would call. There was never a reply. Bruner would then get up and look out into the dimly lit main room. No one was ever visible. Once she heard noises from the office next to hers. "It sounded like books being taken off shelves and then replaced," she said. "I checked, but no one was there."

Bruner would simply shrug and go back to work. After all, it wasn't her first experience with ghosts. She had worked at Fort Missoula from 1983 to 2000, first as an administrative aide, then as Curator of Education. A number of inexplicable things happened during the years she worked there.

"We didn't have a groundskeeper," Bruner recalled, "and there were thirty-two acres to take care of. I was working one Saturday, trying to drive a tractor around and mow. It was a hot summer day, and I was wearing a sleeveless shell and a pair of shorts. At the end of the day, I went downstairs to the basement to turn off the lights. Just as I reached for the switches, I felt a cold hand on my shoulder. I looked around and there was no one there. It scared me half to death. I was up those stairs like a shot.

"Whenever we changed exhibits, particularly if we were doing something about the history of the fort, things would disappear. One of my co-workers, Kathy, was working on a map in the shop down in the basement. She left it on the drawing table for a bit to go upstairs to talk to another woman who was doing some installation. They talked for a little bit, and then, since it was getting late, Kathy went back downstairs to put her stuff away for the day. The map was gone. She came back upstairs and asked if she had left the map upstairs. The other lady told her she hadn't. Kathy could have sworn that she had left the map on the drawing table. At last she gave up and decided to go home. She put on her coat, and when she got to the door, she looked down, and there was the map, propped against the door."

"We found things like hammers up on the rafters," Bruner continued. "My keys disappeared for two months. I looked everywhere, and finally gave up and got new keys. The old keys were found back in the textile room, a storage area for textiles, where I hadn't been for a long time. No one else had borrowed them.

"We used to hear doors opening and shutting a lot. Security wasn't what it is today, but there was never anyone there when we looked. Even after locks were changed and a doorbell put on, we still heard doors.

"And then I had an experience with a gentleman, a black gentleman, when we had an exhibit on the history of Fort Missoula. It was after five o'clock, and I was there alone. I was getting ready to close. The director had gone through the building already and told me that everyone had gone, and then he left. As I was getting ready to turn off the lights, I heard this voice say, 'Oh, are you closing, Ma'am?'

"I turned around and saw a black man. He was dressed in

one of those collarless shirts. He was well-dressed and clean but—oh, I don't know.

"He said, 'Oh, I'm sorry, did I frighten you?'

"I said, 'Well, I didn't think anybody was here. Where were you?'

"He replied, 'I was back there, looking at your pictures of the soldiers. What do you know about the 25th Infantry?'

"I said, 'Oh, isn't that a neat story?' and we started talking about it. We chatted for a little while. At last he said, 'Oh, I should probably let you go. I'm going to leave now. Thank you very much, I really appreciate your telling the story of this black infantry group because they don't often get a lot of the credit they deserve.'

"'Oh, you're welcome,' I replied. He went out and I locked the door behind him. I went up to my office to get my purse and from up there I could hear a flute playing below, like a military song, right outside the window. I went to the window and looked down and I didn't see anything and I thought, 'That guy—oh that is so cool!' I was going to go out and compliment him. I went right back out again. I could still hear the music playing when I went out the door. I went around the corner and nobody was there and there was no car. I walked all the way around the building. It's out in thirty-two acres of flat land and there's no place he could have gotten to in that short time.

"He didn't seem like somebody from this day and age. He was polite, his dress was old-fashioned but new looking, not scruffy like something you'd pick up at a second-hand store. The 25th Infantry band was stationed at Fort Missoula from 1888 to 1898 and the 25th Infantry Bicycle Corps had a musician too, because they did all these bicycle drills.

"I've read about spirits who follow objects, and we had several items on display from the 25th Infantry Bicycle Corps.

I've always suspected that the black gentleman had been a member of the 25th Infantry Bicycle Corps. "I could almost imagine his group waiting for him outside, while he came in and talked to me, and then they marched away, playing music.

"I've read that spirits seem to follow objects that meant something to them. Everybody who works in a museum seems to have a story. And we moved a lot of our stuff out of the building we were in, which was the old Quartermaster's Warehouse, over to the post hospital, and about that time we stopped having so much activity."

Apparently the haunting has subsided in recent years. Bob Brown, director of the museum, has often worked alone late at night, and says that he has heard nothing more than the usual creaking of an old building. Perhaps the Bicycle Corps phantom has ridden away at last, satisfied that the contributions his group made have at last been properly recognized.

The Historical Museum at Fort Missoula includes 13 historic structures and over 17,000 objects. It was established by community effort in 1975 to save what remained of the original Fort Missoula.

GAMBLER'S
REMORSE

NEVADA CITY
c/o Montana Heritage Commission
Virginia City, Montana 59755
406-843-5247

Ghostly Activity Level: Moderate

HISTORY: Nevada City contains around 100 buildings constructed between 1863, when gold was discovered in nearby Alder Gulch, and the early 1900s. A few buildings are original to the site but most were brought in from elsewhere by historians Charles Bovey and his wife Sue to save them from demolition. The Music Hall contains a huge collection of antique organs and music machines. The Nevada City schoolhouse, built in Twin Bridges in 1867, is probably the oldest existing school in the state. One of the few modern replicas is the railroad depot. It was built in 1964, modeled after a much older depot in Bovey's home state of Minnesota.

PHENOMENA: A former guest was heard pacing in one of the upstairs rooms of the Nevada City Hotel. Heavy, booted footsteps were heard along the boardwalk near the rental cabins, and the figure of a man wearing thick eyeglasses was seen in the train depot.

After you explore Virginia City, why not take an adventurous ride on the 1910 steam train over to Nevada City, just a couple of miles away? Unlike Virginia City, which is the county seat of Madison County and very much alive, Nevada City is a museum town. Visitors can explore the 100 historic buildings that were brought to the site by the Boveys over several decades.

A figure thought by some to be Charlie Bovey himself was seen recently by a Montana Heritage Commission employee. "The boss set us to work cleaning and setting up the gift shop in the Nevada City depot," he told me. "It hadn't been open for about ten years. It was a Tuesday around the middle of May. All the artifacts had been moved out to make room for displays. My two fellow employees needed to run up to Virginia City, so I was in the depot by myself. I had my radio with me so I could call my boss if I needed her. There's a storage area off to the side that looks like an old baggage room. Charlie Bovey had it built to look authentic.

"While I was there I started getting a weird feeling. I turned and there was a guy standing in the baggage room door. He was not very tall and he was wearing really thick 'coke bottle'-type eyeglasses and a pair of Dockers-type trousers, maybe a plaid shirt, and a kind of fisherman's cap. He was leaning on the door, looking at me. I took off running, all the way to the highway.

"I called my boss and told her, 'You gotta get over here, there's someone in the depot!'

"The supervisor of maintenance came driving up on a four-wheeler. He's one of my good friends. We went in and didn't find one person. Then my boss showed up. I pointed out where the guy was. The man who does our living history came down later. I described what I saw to him and he said, 'I think you saw Charlie Bovey's ghost.'

"He showed me a photo of Charlie Bovey. The guy I saw wasn't exactly like the photo, but similar. The guy I saw looked older. If it was Charlie, it might have had something to do with reopening the depot. Maybe he wanted to make sure we were doing things right. That's the kind of guy he was. He was a brilliant historian, and he used his fortune to preserve all these historic buildings."

The man with the thick eyeglasses hasn't been seen since. If it was Charlie Bovey, who devoted his life to preserving Montana's historical buildings, perhaps he was satisfied that his legacy is in good hands.

An overnight guest at the Nevada City Hotel got a little more than he bargained for a few years ago. The hotel, originally built in the 1860s, is known far and wide for its two-story outhouse, one of the few remaining in the United States. The hotel is still open in the summer to guests, who can book rooms above the ladies' parlor and the saloon. Apparently the hotel is haunted. Chris Roberts of Billings had an unforgettable experience there one summer night in 1996. Tired from a long day's drive, his parents retired early to their room upstairs, but Roberts decided to sit on the balcony for a while, idly watching an approaching thunderstorm.

"Lightning streaked across the sky as night set in," he recalled. "The wind picked up and rain began to speckle the wooden sidewalks in front of the old hotel. It soon turned to a downpour. As evening turned to night, the rain let up a bit and the hotel's guests began to settle down for the night. I finally went to my room. It seemed stuffy so I opened the window to let in fresh air. The drapes moved slightly in the breeze, casting eerie shadows on the wall. It seemed like one of those nights when anything could happen.

"I first heard the footsteps as the clock in the saloon downstairs struck three in the morning. The footsteps were in my room, directly in front of me, crossing from one side to the other. I sat up in bed, unsure if what I heard was real. No one was visible, but I could sense the presence of an angry man, pacing impatiently back and forth. I had the impression that he had been cheated at the faro tables in the saloon downstairs. Almost as soon as I realized that, the ghost was gone."

The rest of the night passed quietly. Roberts mentioned the footsteps the next morning, but none of the other guests appeared to have been disturbed.

If you plan to spend a night at the Nevada City Hotel, why not ask for Chris Roberts' room, second from the back on the left? Perhaps you too will have an encounter with the ghost of a cardsharp's victim! Or rent one of the cabins behind the hotel. Heavy, booted footsteps have been heard on the boardwalk when no one is visible. And do step into the depot. If you see an elderly man wearing thick glasses who is there one moment and gone the next, don't worry—it may be Charlie Bovey, just keeping an eye on things.

CHICO'S GHOSTLY FACE

CHICO HOT SPRINGS LODGE
1 Chico Road
Pray, Montana 59065
406-333-4933

Ghostly Activity Level: High

HISTORY: Chico Hot Springs Hotel was built in 1900 by gold miner Bill Knowles and his wife Percie. Bill died in 1910, and Percie, who had always opposed the use of liquor, quickly closed the hotel's saloon and turned the building into a health resort. Chico's fame spread quickly under the direction of Dr. George Townsend, and a hospital wing, laboratory, operating room, and a suite of examination rooms were soon added. Business declined during the 1930s Depression and Percie's health eventually broke under the financial strain. No longer able to take part in running the operation, she spent much of her time sitting in a rocking chair in what is now Room 349, staring out the window. In 1936 she was committed to the state insane asylum at Warm Springs. She died there a few years later. The hotel changed hands a number of times over the succeeding years. Chico Hot Springs Resort now attracts visitors from all over the world.

PHENOMENA: Percie Knowles has made her presence

known on a number of occasions. In 1986 two security guards saw a filmy "something" hovering above the piano and managed to photograph it. Also, guards have seen Percie and Bill sitting at a table by the window in the bar. Dogs sometimes appear to watch something invisible to us crossing the lobby. Guests in Room 351 were awakened one night by the sweet scent of jasmine perfume and saw a dark figure standing at the foot of their bed.

I arrived at Chico Hot Springs Resort with my friend Frank on Presidents' Day weekend. The original lodge was fully booked, so we were lodged in one of the newer buildings. We dropped off our luggage and hurried over to the main lodge, eager to explore the scene of the haunting. The lodge is an impressive three-story white clapboard building set at the foot of snowcapped Emigrant Peak. The lobby was crowded; several guests had their dogs. I watched them with particular interest, for dogs sometimes behave strangely in haunted buildings. These, however, just sat quietly beside their owners. Perhaps there was too much bustle for a shy ghost to make her appearance, or too early in the evening. I knew most of the sightings had taken place late at night, after the saloon had closed and the hotel was quiet.

I introduced myself to Sue, the desk clerk, who had formerly worked as the night auditor, and asked about the haunting. She told me she had often felt watched at night, and that objects occasionally disappeared when her back was turned. Once a stack of paperwork had vanished completely, only to turn up on the front seat of her co-worker's locked car the next morning.

One of her co-workers actually saw the ghost while she was working on the third floor late one night. The ghost's features were distinct, definitely resembling photographs of

Percie with her hair drawn back in a bun. Although the ghost did not seem to be aware of her, the employee was terrified and ran downstairs to the lobby. Sue had no doubt that the worker had actually seen something, for her face was ashen and she was badly shaken.

"Do dogs seem to react to the ghosts?" I asked.

The desk clerk nodded. "At night I often bring my dog to work, and at times she will turn her head as though she is watching something invisible cross the lobby." Then she showed me a copy of a letter from a Wyoming couple who had stayed at Chico in 1996. They had slept in room 351, next to the room in which Percie had spent several years toward the end of her life. They were disturbed several times during the night by noises coming from the roof and the sound of a key being repeatedly jiggled in the lock. One time they awakened to find a shadow standing at the foot of the bed, and the husband noticed a sweet perfume, possibly jasmine. They claimed to have known nothing of the haunting beforehand.

The next morning I asked whether I could visit Room 349. I was given two large, old-fashioned keys to unlock rooms 349 and 351. We walked down the narrow hallway past two maids tidying a room, and unlocked 349. It proved a small room, comfortable, distinguished from nearby rooms only by its lovely view of the nearby mountains. The maids had obviously just cleaned the room, so we were careful not to disturb anything. After taking a number of photos with Polaroid and 35mm cameras, we carefully locked the door and moved next door.

Room 351 is larger, with two beds, and windows on two sides that flood the room with a pleasant golden light. It didn't look the least bit ghostly, at least in broad daylight. We followed the same procedure, taking photos with both cameras, and then left, relocking the room.

On a whim, I decided to go back into Room 349 to finish off my roll of film. I unlocked the door and stepped inside. I heard a slight gasp, as if I had surprised someone. Almost reflexively I raised my 35mm and took three quick snapshots from slightly different angles. At the same time, Frank exclaimed, "The bedspread's wrinkled!"

And so it was. When we had locked the room ten minutes earlier and gone next door, the bedspread had been perfectly smooth, exactly as the maids had left it. Now there were wrinkles in the middle, just as if someone had sat on the bed.

Had I disturbed Percie? I can only state that the bedspread was smooth when we left the room earlier and it was now undeniably wrinkled.

We went down to the front desk to return the keys and I mentioned the wrinkles, adding that we had been especially careful not to disturb anything. Had anything like that been reported before?

The answer was no. Apparently this was a first. If the staff at the front desk doubted our story, however, they were far too gracious to say so!

When my 35mm photographs were developed, they showed something odd: the gradual materialization of what may be a woman's face. The first snapshot shows an odd patch of light on the wall. On the second, a hazy face seems to be forming. The face is clearer in the third photo, and bears a resemblance to Percie, complete with upswept hairstyle.

Is it really Percie's ghost, or just a flaw on the wall? I recalled the many sightings of the ghost over the years, and the faint gasp I thought I heard in Percie's old room, and wondered...

Postscript: In the summer of 2000, Percie materialized in

the dining room in full view of guests. And in 2002, two young women who had booked one of the rooms on the third floor were awakened several times when the door of their room opened by itself. The corridor outside their room was empty— or so it seemed.

You'll enjoy Chico's wonderful hot springs, fabulous dining, and wide variety of outdoor activities. Perhaps you'll even be one of the fortunate guests to have a truly out-of-this world adventure!

THE GUEST WHO NEVER CHECKED OUT

POLLARD HOTEL
2 North Broadway
Red Lodge, Montana 59068
406-446-0001

Ghostly Activity Level: High

HISTORY: The Pollard Hotel was built in 1893, the first brick building in the bustling coal-mining town of Red Lodge. Known at first as the Spofford Hotel, its guests included frontiersman Liver-Eatin' Johnston as well as celebrities such as Buffalo Bill Cody and Calamity Jane. Now listed in the National Register of Historic Places, the Pollard draws tourists from all over the world who brave the switchbacks of the Beartooth Highway en route to Yellowstone National Park in summer, and skiers who come to enjoy some of Montana's best powder skiing at nearby Red Lodge Mountain in winter.

PHENOMENA: The scent of a fine French perfume is sometimes noticed on the second floor. Lights are found on in empty rooms, and the unmistakable sound of a racquetball game in progress has been heard from darkened, locked courts. Staff have seen the figure of a paunchy man in 1920s-era "plus four" golfing trousers, on the main stairs and also pouring himself a cup of coffee in the main bar. A photo taken by a guest shows the faint image of a woman with shoulder-length dark hair, a white blouse, and a 1940s jumper.

Like most fine hotels, the Pollard takes justifiable pride in its elegant décor, attentive but unobtrusive service, and long tradition of fine cuisine. Guests are often reluctant to leave the comfort of the Pollard, and a few, apparently, enjoyed their stay so much that they have never checked out. Their spirits are said to linger in the hotel's quiet corridors and rooms. The Pollard, like many historic hotels, is haunted.

In October my friend Jeannette and I drove to Red Lodge to find the town digging out from under 15 inches of snow. After an excellent lunch, we settled ourselves in the Pollard's History Room to examine scrapbooks filled with clippings about the hotel. An article entitled "Friendly Ghost Remains at Pollard Hotel" from the *Carbon County News* of October 26, 1994, described a number of reputed encounters with the Pollard's ghost. There are at least three: a lady in Victorian clothes, a small boy who sometimes accompanies her, and a male ghost called George.

"George" apparently spends much of his time in Room 114, where handprints are sometimes found on the mirror, and Room 214, where the door often closes by itself despite being propped open while housekeepers clean the room. The appetizing smell of fresh coffee or popcorn has also been noted in those rooms, even when they have been unoccupied for several days.

According to staff, "George" also likes to tinker with electrical devices, setting off all the smoke alarms at once or causing all the hotel's telephones to ring at the same time. Footsteps are sometimes heard going up and down the stairs when the hotel is closed. A female employee has even glimpsed "George" on two occasions, on the landing of the staircase in the lobby, and again in the bar, pouring himself a cup of coffee. He looked solid and seemed quite at home. She described him as a man in his sixties, pot-bellied, and wearing "plus fours," which were popular from about 1890 to the 1930s. He vanished almost before she realized what she had seen.

We had made arrangements for a tour of the hotel with one of the staff who preferred to remain anonymous. She greeted us cordially and took us into the Gallery, a three-story atrium featuring a huge stained-glass window, a massive fireplace, and many comfortable chairs and sofas. The Gallery was built in 1992 around an outdoor laundry area that had been the site of a number of strange happenings. On the second floor, she pointed out the two rooms where housekeeping staff had sensed the ghostly presence. No one knew who "George" might have been, but he was obviously a gentleman at heart, for whenever those rooms were occupied, "George" obligingly moved out.

Our guide left us briefly to answer a question from another employee, and I strolled over to a window to admire the view of the snow-covered Beartooth Mountains in the distance. As I turned back, I caught a tantalizing whiff of perfume. It was a delicate floral scent, quite lovely, and not one that I recognized. Jeannette noticed it too.

"It reminds me of my grandmother's French perfume," Jeannette remarked. Had the Pollard's Victorian lady ghost decided to make her presence felt? Then Jeannette gave an exclamation and pointed to the basket of potpourri standing in the corner a few feet away. I leaned over and sniffed at it. The potpourri had a woodsy odor, with a slightly spicy overtone, nothing at all like the delightful floral scent that by then was no longer detectable. Had that ethereal scent really come from a potpourri mix? The verdict could only be "Not proven."

Encouraged nevertheless, we followed the staff member down the corridor to Room 210, where lights sometimes switched themselves back on as soon as housekeeping staff left the room. The lights were definitely off. Perhaps "George" had tired of the game. Then we went up to the third floor, where we examined yet another room said to be haunted. It had a peculiar quality of stillness about it that I had encountered in other haunted places, a sense that beneath the bustle of modern-day life, traces of the past still lingered. It might have been interesting to spend a night in that room, but we had a long snowy drive ahead of us, and we wanted to get back to Billings while the sun was still shining.

The Pollard still hosts a lively assortment of ghosts. Not long ago a group of businessmen and their wives spent a weekend at the Pollard. They knew nothing about the haunting, yet one of the women noticed the scent of a fine perfume in one of the second-floor corridors. She wasn't wearing perfume at the time, and the corridor was empty.

In November 2003, guest Sue Tracy felt strangely uneasy on the landing of the stairway where George had been seen. A photo taken by fellow guest Frank Stevens just then shows the head and shoulders of a woman with shoulder-length dark hair, a white blouse, and the wide straps of a 1940s-era jumper floating just behind Tracy.

A week later, paranormal investigator Richard Worden happened to be at the Pollard with two friends. They were quietly talking in the atrium about 10:30 p.m. when all three of them saw what they described as "a shimmer in the air" pass nearby. At the same time, Worden caught a strong whiff of shaving lotion.

"It looked like a veil, rippling past us," Worden told me. "We all saw it."

Later that same night, they met in one of their bedrooms

on the third floor to discuss what they had seen. All of a sudden the door began to rattle, and then very slowly it opened. All three men got up. Worden walked over to the door and stepped out into the hall.

"There's no one here," he told his friends, and turned to go back in. At that moment an unseen presence walked right through him. His friends saw Worden's eyes widen and knew that something strange had happened, although none of them saw anything unusual.

I couldn't resist asking Worden what it felt like to have a ghost walk through him.

"It felt really weird," he replied after a moment's thought. "Like someone had opened a door in my chest and walked through me."

Worden mentioned his experience to the receptionist at the front desk. The man didn't seem at all surprised. "You ought to be here on New Year's or St. Pat's Day," he told Worden. "The ghosts really get active around then."

So who are the ghosts of the Pollard? Perhaps they are former townspeople, still celebrating New Year's Eve or St. Patrick's Day as they used to. Perhaps they are former staff who never really retired, or guests from long ago who are reluctant to leave the comforts of this historic hotel. If so, who could blame them? I too, was reluctant to leave.

The Pollard offers thoroughly modern rooms, fine dining, and possibly a chance encounter with one of the hotel's phantoms. Stunning views of the Beartooth Mountains and a stroll through the historic streets of Red Lodge will make your visit even more enjoyable.

THE NOTORIOUS
MILFORD PRICE

HOTEL MONTANA
Reed Point, Montana 59069
406-326-2288

Ghostly Activity Level: Moderate

HISTORY: The Hotel Montana was built in 1909 as a general merchandise store that sold everything from clothing to farm machinery. In later years, the second floor was divided into single rooms for long-term boarders. Russ and Connie Schlievert bought the two-story brick building in 1994. Long-time antiques dealers, they had dreamed of someday owning a 1900s-era saloon and a bed-and-breakfast inn where they could display some of their antiques. After more than a year of hard work, the old store re-opened as the Hotel Montana. The Wild Horse Saloon now occupies the first floor, with several bedrooms plus a comfortable sitting room on the second floor.

PHENOMENA: Russ Schlievert and the former owners of the building saw the ghost of a tall, thin man thought to be Milford Price, who was killed just outside the hotel in 1932. Guests commented on inexplicable cold spots on the second floor and the creaking of floorboards at night, as if someone unseen were pacing around just outside Room 4.

The June morning was already warm as I drove slowly down Reed Point's six-block-long main street. The lone bicyclist I passed seemed strangely out of place in a town that looked like a stage set for a Western movie, with its board sidewalks and false-fronted buildings. It wasn't at all difficult to believe that a ghost or two might choose to linger here in such a peaceful setting.

In 1909, Reed Point was a bustling town with over 3,000 residents. At the time, it was confidently predicted that the town would someday rival Billings as a shipping hub. During the economic depression of the 1930s, Reed Point's fortunes declined, and the population gradually shrank. Today, the town has just over 100 residents.

In 1989, during the celebrations of Montana's centennial, Reed Point found itself unexpectedly in the international spotlight. The little town's wild and woolly Running of the Sheep, modeled after the Running of the Bulls in Pamplona, Spain, was a huge success. What had started out as a good-natured poke at the hoopla surrounding the Great Centennial Cattle Drive brought more than 12,000 visitors from all over the world. The event was a rousing success and still attracts thousands of visitors each Labor Day weekend.

Reed Point has had a few dark moments in its history, though. On December 29, 1932, a shocking event occurred just outside the building that is now the Hotel Montana. Newspapers all over the state carried the dramatic tale of extortion, murder, and swift justice. According to Russ and Connie Schlievert, owners of the Hotel Montana, the reverberations of that event can still be felt today.

Connie greeted us pleasantly at the door of the substantial two-story brick hotel. After I introduced my friends Frank and Sue and explained that we had come in search of ghosts, she suggested we go upstairs and look around while she went to fetch her husband Russ. "He's a skeptic," she said, "but he's seen the ghost twice outside of Room 4 and he can tell you the story."

The three of us paused to admire the saloon, with its gorgeous tin ceiling, and then made our way upstairs to the second floor. A long hallway opened onto a cozy sitting area surrounded by bedrooms. Sue headed straight for the colorful "Madam's Room," furnished with crimson draperies and rose-colored ceiling tiles, while Frank paused to take photos of the sitting area. I stepped into Room 4, a large and pleasant room with a ceiling fan. An assortment of Victorian costumes is hung up and ready for guests who want to totally immerse themselves in the late nineteenth century. I walked over to the window to look out, and found myself pushing through a swirling column of cold air. Although there was a ceiling fan, it was not on at the time. I had a feeling that a night in this room could prove interesting.

Russ Schlievert came upstairs soon afterward. He gave us a tour of the second floor, pointing out where the old sheriff's office had been, and where he had discovered a hidden room, once a lawyer's office, when they ripped out a wall. He and his wife had done most of the remodeling work themselves, often working late in the evenings.

"The first time I saw the ghost was in 1994," he said. "It was maybe eleven-thirty, twelve at night. I was up here tearing lath and plaster out of that room. I had a wheelbarrow here, and I'd haul stuff down the hall to the window and dump it down the chute outside. Well, I felt somebody behind me and thought it was my wife. I turned my head and saw a man wearing a tunic coat, a black coat down to his knees, and wire-rimmed glasses; he was real tall and thin with a real shiny face. When I turned around to see who it was, he took about three steps like this"—Russ took three exaggeratedly long steps, as a man might if he were trying to sneak away without being noticed—"and disappeared.

"Fern and Bill Baker, who ran the place when it was a store from 1944 to 1970, were out here a few weeks later. I asked her if she ever had anything strange happen to her. And I told her about the ghost.

"'Oh, he's not to be worried about,' she said. 'That's Milford Price. He was here all the time we were here.' She went on to say that when freight would come in downstairs, if it were left there a couple of days, they'd find it had been moved to the other side of the building. Another owner had heard all kinds of strange noises, but she never saw the ghost. She ran the place for about six years."

Guests at the Hotel Montana have also had some ghostly encounters. "When we opened," Russ told us, "we had some people from Ireland staying here. The next morning they asked me if I ever had any strange cold feelings outside the door of Room 4. They didn't know anything about a ghost. I've had four other people stay in Room 4 and ask me who was out in the hall last night. When you're in that room at night you'll hear these floorboards outside the door squeaking, and there's no one here.

"I tell guests about Milford Price, but we don't really know if it is him. He homesteaded about seven miles off the road, and he was a real scoundrel. In the thirties, people didn't always spend the winter on their homesteads. They were supposed to, but sometimes they'd cheat and come into town instead. When they would go out to their homestead in the spring, stuff would be gone. They'd go over to the Price homestead and there would be their plow, their wagon, their buggy, or their pitchfork. It was a wonder he never got shot before the sheriff got him.

"Well, there's a story that a young kid came to town. He had a Model T, painted red, and they pushed it off the train at the siding, and he drove around town looking for work. Someone sent him to Milford Price because Price was looking for a ranch hand. Last time they ever saw the kid. A couple weeks later, Price was seen driving the kid's Model T.

"Anyway, Price took that Model T and went to Rapelje and talked to the banker there. The story is that he wanted to mortgage the cows that were on his place. There was quite a herd of cows out there, sixty, seventy head maybe, so the banker gave him the $2,500 to buy the two homesteads next to his. Before Price even got back to Reed Point, the banker found out that the cows on the place weren't Milford's cows. They were there on shares. Anyway, the banker gets on the telegraph and the telegraph man ran up to the sheriff's office right here in this building.

"The sheriff heard the Model T pull up across the street, and called out the window, 'Milford, you stand right there, we want to talk to you about this bank deal in Rapelje.' According to court records, Milford gave the sheriff a hand signal, might have been the old bird, and took off running. The sheriff yelled for him to halt, but Milford ran between this building and the livery stable next door. The sheriff grabbed his shotgun off the wall and ran down the corridor to this window. Milford was trying to climb over a fence when the sheriff shot him in the back.

"When Milford's ranch was sold, the people who bought it had well trouble. Six, seven months later, they took the boards off the bottom of the windmill, and there in a shallow grave was the body of the boy who owned the Model T."

Over 70 years had passed since Price's death, and people's recollection of events fades with time. I was curious to find out just how much the story had changed since the shooting, so I looked up the original reports of the shooting in the *Billings Gazette* and Helena's *Independent Record* for December 30 and 31, 1932. Price had indeed tried to extort money from William J. Sodderlind, president of the First National Bank of Rapelje. The banker had received a letter on December 19 demanding $1,000, but ignored it. On December 23, he received another, instructing him to bring $1,500 to the filling station in Reed Point and leave it in his car between six and eight P.M. on the night of December 29. Sodderlind had showed the letter to Sheriff Jack Benjamin, who advised him to follow the instructions. Meanwhile, the sheriff set up a trap. When Price opened the car door that night and reached for the currency, the sheriff, who had hidden in a nearby building, ordered him to halt. Instead, Price dashed for cover. Sheriff Benjamin and deputy game warden Herman Falor called out warnings, but Price wouldn't stop. Both men fired, and slugs from their shotguns riddled Price's body. He died at a local hospital a few minutes later.

So far, local legend had proven pretty accurate, but there was no mention in the articles about a young man with a red Model T. Curiously, though, a year later the *Independent Record* carried a follow-up story entitled "Big Timber Sheriff Continues Probe in Disappearance of A. M. Mitchell." When Milford Price's automobile had been examined, bloodstains were on the rear seat cushions. Price had been working with a farmhand, 45-year-old Albert M. Mitchell, who had mysteriously disappeared in December 1932, about two weeks before Price was killed. The automobile turned out to have belonged to Mitchell. It was noted in the article that the Yellowstone River had not been frozen at the time of Mitchell's disappearance. If Price actually murdered Mitchell, it would have been easy to dispose of the body in the river. No trace of Mitchell was ever found.

Milford Price died just outside the Hotel Montana. If the ghost who haunts the hotel is indeed Milford Price, perhaps the reason he paces up and down the corridor outside Room 4 can be explained by his last words: "I'm so sorry," he is reported to have sobbed just before he died. "I don't know why I did that."

He has eternity to think about it.

The Hotel Montana is perfect for those who enjoy historic surroundings. Guests can choose from an assortment of Victorian costumes and enjoy live music in the Wild Horse Saloon downstairs. Guests may also be offered entertainment of a different sort, courtesy of Milford Price. If you should hear the floorboards outside your bedroom door creak during the night and look out to see a tall, thin man disappear down the hallway, don't worry—it's probably just Milford, eternally fleeing the sheriff.

SHERIFF HENRY PLUMMER
AND MORE

VIRGINIA CITY
c/o Montana Heritage Commission
Virginia City, Montana 59755
406-843-5247

Ghostly Activity Level: High

HISTORY: In 1863, gold was discovered in Alder Gulch. Thousands of miners rushed to Montana hoping to strike it rich. Several small settlements sprang up to cater to them, strung out along a 14-mile stretch of the gulch. At its peak Virginia City was the largest, with a population of over 10,000. In 1865, Virginia City became the capital of Montana Territory. By 1868, the easily accessible gold was gone and most of the miners had left for richer diggings in Helena. Unlike most mining towns, however, Virginia City was never abandoned. Dredges and hydraulic mining brought in enough gold to keep the town alive. After World War II, however, Virginia City's fortunes declined and at one point was in danger of being abandoned. In 1953, Montana ranchers Charles and Sue Bovey began the long process of preserving the deteriorating old buildings. In 1997, the Montana legislature purchased the restored buildings at Virginia City and nearby Nevada City from the Bovey family. The buildings are now in the care of the Montana Heritage Commission. Because Virginia City contains so many examples of Victorian architecture, many Western movies have been filmed there. The town was declared a National Historic Landmark in 1961.

PHENOMENA: Employees of the Wells Fargo Coffee House heard a woman singing early in the morning. At the Bonanza Inn, once a Catholic hospital but now used to house summer employees, a mischievous ghost sometimes unmakes beds, hides towels, and knocks on doors. The ghost of a little girl was seen sitting on the front steps of a building used to store costumes and props for the Virginia City Players. Employees and guests at the Bennett House bed and breakfast inn often report mysterious footsteps upstairs.

I arrived in Virginia City on a sunny August morning to find the town bustling with tourists in shorts and t-shirts. Many of them were clustered around the train station, waiting for the 1910 Baldwin steam locomotive to arrive from nearby Nevada City. Others were taking photos of two ladies wearing Victorian riding habits who had paused to rest their Arabian horses in the shade of a tree. A pair of re-enactors in 1860s Army uniforms strolled down the boardwalk, eyeing the saucily dressed saloon girls who beckoned to them from the Bale of Hay Saloon. I caught snatches of German, French, and languages I didn't recognize as I squeezed through the crowds with my friends Frank and Sue.

My object was to interview some of the folks who leased stores from the state for the summer, to see whether they had experienced paranormal activity. Virginia City has been called the ghost capital of Montana, but it soon became obvious that many of the merchants preferred to downplay the ghost stories. One man who agreed to share his experiences asked me not to identify his store, because he was worried that visitors might not want to come into a business known to be haunted.

"On occasion I stay in here at night," he told me. "A couple of times I've been awakened by noise in the front area, sounded like tin cans rattling, and it's quiet here at night, so just about any noise will wake you up. Tin cans rattling up in the corner, and there's no tin cans in this corner, let alone rattling. Another time it sounded like a trunk opening in the back corner. So it's only been twice, and I've slept here a lot of times. It sounded like a trunk opening and closing, and there's no trunk here.

"Before that happened, I'd hear footsteps, like someone in boots was walking up the sidewalk, and I'd get up and look, and nobody would be in sight. It was probably three or four in the morning. One time I had my oldest son walk up and down on the boardwalk and it sounded the same. I've had this store eight years, and it's only happened two or three times."

A college student who worked as a clerk in another store told me that when business was slow he would sometimes pull out a paperback and read, to pass the time until another customer came in. "Sometimes I'd get so engrossed in my novel that I'd forget to watch for customers," he said. "And then I would hear a man clear his throat, like he was trying to get my attention. When I looked up, though, there was never anyone there. A couple of other times I heard footsteps shuffling around at the back of the store. There's no place for anyone to hide, and I never saw anyone."

Perhaps the footsteps heard by various shopkeepers belonged to the figure seen by J. P. Johnson one night. Johnson is another of the many college students who work at Virginia City during the summer. Late one evening he was on his way back to the trailer in which he lived when he happened to notice a tall man wearing a soldier's coat leaning up against a lamppost about 200 feet away, smoking a cigarette. Johnson thought little of it, since there are often re-enactors in military uniform at Virginia City. It seemed an odd place for the man to be, however, since the re-enactors were billeted elsewhere in town. Johnson turned to get a better look at him but the man was nowhere to be seen. "There was no way that he could have gotten out of sight so quickly," Johnson said. "Lately I'd been thinking of Jack Gallagher, the sheriff's deputy who was hanged by the Vigilance Committee. Maybe it was Gallagher's ghost I saw." Gallagher was among five men accused of being members of a robber band, hanged on January 14, 1864.

Another candidate might be George Ives, hanged on December 21, 1863, for the murder of Nicholas Tabalt. In her memoirs, Mary Ronan, who lived in Virginia City at the time, describes Ives as tall, and usually dressed in a long blue soldier's overcoat.

Visitors who want to try their luck at having a ghostly encounter might book a room at the Bennett House bed-and-breakfast inn. This building was formerly the home of Judge J. A. Bennett, and guests have reported eerie occurrences. Jeff and Natalie, a young couple who spend most of each summer as re-enactors at Virginia City, often stay at the Bennett House. One morning, as Natalie was walking alone along a corridor, she heard a man's voice behind her, saying something she didn't quite catch. She turned to see who was speaking. No one was there. Another young woman reportedly felt someone invisible sit down on the side of her bed. Guests have heard footsteps coming from an unoccupied bedroom. It's thought that the ghosts may be those of Judge Bennett and his wife, keeping an eye on their old home.

Paranormal activity at the Wells Fargo Coffee House, once the S. R. Buford Store, convinced chef Amy Millsap that ghosts really do exist. On July 6, 1997, *Montana Standard* reporter Perry Backus reported in an article entitled "Ghost Stories Thrive in Spooky Virginia City Haunts" that Millsap heard a woman singing in the dining room after the coffee house closed one night. She thought someone had left the tape player on and went in to shut it off, but found it wasn't on. Another employee was baking muffins at the coffee house one morning when she heard a woman sobbing. The crying woman could not be located.

The Bonanza Inn, sometimes used to house state employees, is also haunted. The ghost seems to be a young nun who appears to people who are ill and tends to them. The building, at first used as the county courthouse, became a hospital run by the Sisters of Charity in the mid-1870s. It now is used to house summer employees. Both the Bonanza Inn and the Bonanza House, once home to the nuns, are haunted. Phenomena reported by those who have stayed in the buildings include rapping on doors and windows, the apparition of a young nun, mysterious voices, items strewn around rooms when no one was present, and the appearance of a male ghost wearing nineteenth-century clothing.

The Opera House is yet another building where echoes from the past are sometimes heard. One year, employees working late at night to prepare the Opera House for a new summer season reported phantom footsteps and a man's laughter. And the ghost of a little blonde girl in an old-fashioned dress has been seen many times near the costume shop. She is thought to be one of the pioneer children, perhaps a victim of an epidemic.

The rehearsal hall behind the theater is also haunted, according to Gerry Roe, now a professor in the theater department at Rocky Mountain College in Billings. One summer he played the part of the barber in *The Demon Barber*. At the time, actors were billeted in the basement of the rehearsal hall. On several occasions Roe heard footsteps cross the main floor when he knew no one else was in the building. "After the first time I would go up and look around, but I never saw anybody and all the lights were off. The footsteps didn't sound like modern shoes. There was nothing soft about them. They could have been cowboy boots," he told me.

By the time we had explored most of the buildings along Wallace Street, it was time for lunch. The three of us ordered a pizza at the busy Bale of Hay Saloon and found a table at the back, as far away from the honky-tonk piano player as possible. Never comfortable in crowds at the best of times, I suddenly felt overwhelmed by the noise and the bustle. "I've got to get out of here," I urgently told Frank and Sue. I'd intended to stay another hour or two, but the need to leave had become imperative, even if it meant abandoning our half-eaten pizza. I simply couldn't handle the crowds any longer. Frank and Sue looked a bit disappointed, but it was with a feeling of great relief that I climbed back into our van and drove out of Virginia City.

When I played back the taped interview with the merchant who had slept in his store, I heard something odd: "There's stuff that goes on here," he had said at the end of the interview. A moment later, a whispery male voice added feelingly, "*Too* much!"

There had been no one within at least a dozen feet of us, yet it sounded as though the voice was directly in front of my tape recorder. Perhaps one of Virginia City's phantoms shared my dislike of crowds, and my sudden, overwhelming urge to leave wasn't completely my own after all.

Virginia City offers a wide variety of things to do and see. You might enjoy a ride in an old stagecoach that is sometimes held up by road agents, or follow a costumed guide on an evening's ghost tour. If you're fortunate, you may catch a glimpse of a tall shadowy figure wearing a soldier's coat, or hear heavy bootsteps on the boardwalk when no one is visible.

THE MAN IN THE
DERBY HAT

BELTON CHALET
P.O. Box 206
West Glacier, Montana 59502
1-888-235-8665

Ghostly Activity Level: High

HISTORY: In 1910, the Great Northern Railway built a Swiss-style chalet to house tourists who came by rail to visit the newly dedicated Glacier National Park. Two cottages were built next, and then a large lodge in 1913. Guests could explore Glacier by stagecoach, lake steamers, or on horseback, and return at night to the comfort of a blazing fire and excellent cuisine. During World War II, travel for pleasure declined and the lodge was closed. Gradually the chalet deteriorated. In 1993, Andy Baxter and Cas Still bought the chalet, installed modern plumbing and heating, and brought the building back to its former grandeur. It is now a National Historic Landmark.

PHENOMENA: Paranormal phenomena have been noted in most of the buildings of the Belton Chalet complex as well as at the train station across the street. At the original chalet, now a restaurant, the ghost of a man wearing a derby hat and carrying a satchel was seen. Doors mysteriously unlock after employees lock them for the night, and the heavy door of the walk-in cooler was heard opening and closing by itself. At night in the lodge, phantom footsteps echo on wood floors, the heartbroken sobbing of a woman was heard, and water faucets turn on and off by themselves. The ghost of the man in the derby hat was seen outside the train station and at the lodge. Employees have heard their names called when no one is near.

We arrived at Belton Chalet late one afternoon, just as a chilly drizzle began to fall. Wraiths of mist were slowly descending the slopes of the nearby mountains, and wind carried the scent of fresh snow from the highest peaks even though it was only mid-August. It looked like a perfect night to curl up in chairs around a blazing fire and tell ghost stories. There was even a chance that the three of us—Frank, Sue, and I—might have an adventure of our very own at what is without a doubt one of the most haunted sites in Montana.

There were no elevators in this nearly century-old lodge, so we carried our luggage up the stairs and along the creaking corridor. The most-haunted room, Number 37, was already occupied, but we had managed to secure rooms 31 and 35. The rooms turned out to be spacious, if rustic, with comfortable beds and private baths. There were no telephones or televisions to distract from the beautiful scenery outside the windows. I stood for a moment staring at the dripping forest behind the lodge and wondered how many other guests over the long years had stood in that spot, gazing at the same scenery. For a moment the past seemed very close.

According to chalet staff, a search through old records revealed no tragic events that might account for the haunting. There are local legends, of course: a man was killed by a train across the street from the chalet, a woman despondent over a love affair threw herself from a ledge behind the buildings, the chalet was built on an Indian burial ground. So far, however, no historical basis for the haunting has been found.

Guests aren't told about the haunting when they check in because the staff doesn't want to frighten anyone, but it's certainly not a secret. Several newspaper and magazine accounts of the haunting are prominently displayed on the walls of the game room in the basement and in the second-floor corridor.

Christie Roberts, general manager of the lodge, had agreed to meet us after dinner and share some of her experiences. Since the restaurant wouldn't open until five, we decided to explore the lodge from the creaking top-floor corridor to the huge stone fireplace near the front desk to the game room in the basement. By then the drizzle had settled into a light rain, and hikers were beginning to straggle in, wet and muddy. Just before five, we went back upstairs to our rooms to grab our jackets. Barely a minute later I heard Sue knock urgently at our door.

"The hot water was running in my sink! I'm sure it was off when I left."

I followed her into her room and touched the taps. Sue had turned off the faucet, but it still felt very hot, indicating that it had been running for a long time. Fortunately, the sink had not overflowed. Sue's belongings had not been disturbed and there was no sign that anyone had been in her room.

We decided to report what appeared to be a problem with the plumbing, only to hear the lady ahead of us at the front desk report that the same thing had happened in her room just down the hall from Sue's.

"There was no damage," she assured the desk clerk. "It didn't overflow."

The clerk nodded. "We've been getting a lot of that this

year," she said matter-of-factly.

When the other guest had moved out of earshot, I told the clerk that Sue had found her water running too, and asked bluntly, "What's causing it? Is it just old plumbing?"

It wasn't old plumbing. According to the clerk, the plumbing had been updated when the building was renovated just a few years before. Lately, though, a number of guests had found water running in their sinks or, conversely, that the water had been shut off at the valve beneath the sink. In each case the room had been locked and unoccupied at the time. It had happened too often to be mere forgetfulness on the part of guests.

"We think it's a mischievous ghost," the clerk said. She hadn't experienced anything unusual herself, but a previous female guest in Room 30 had reported a woman weeping despondently in her room all night. "I didn't know how to comfort her, so I started praying for her," the guest told management the next day. "I couldn't see anything but I could feel her and hear the weeping." A night auditor also heard the weeping late one winter night. It seemed to come from Room 37. He was the only person in the lodge that night.

"And one guest said he was touched on the shoulder as he sat up in bed," the clerk added helpfully. I couldn't help but shiver at the thought. All of a sudden, snuggling up in a warm bed didn't seem as appealing as usual!

It was nearly five o'clock by then, so we hurried through the rain to the nearby restaurant. That building, now the Tap Inn, was the original Belton Chalet, built in 1910. Christie Roberts arrived just as we finished an excellent dinner. She had brought financial manager Mary Pete. The two women spend the winter by themselves at Belton Chalet, keeping an eye on things. They are well aware of the ghostly activity that seems to intensify in the autumn, and take it in stride.

"There may be as many as six ghosts," Roberts told me. "There's a man wearing a derby hat who's been seen in Room 37 and at the train station. Guests have heard doors slamming and ghostly voices calling their names."

During renovation in 1998, a number of odd things happened to the work crews. Mary Pete's husband brought their dog to keep him company one day, and he noticed the dog was sitting at the foot of the stairs staring intently at the landing. No one was visible, but suddenly a child's marble came bouncing down the stairs. "My husband picked it up," Pete said. "It was an old Chinese marble. We still have it at the lodge."

Strange things continued to happen during the renovation. Furniture would move around by itself, and muffled noises were heard coming from empty rooms. On one occasion, black soot was found covering walls that had just been painted, soot that resembled the smudges left by kerosene lanterns. No explanation was ever found.

Pete herself has had a number of strange experiences. "Once I was moving furniture on the second floor of the chalet and was locked into the bathroom. I couldn't open the door. Christie had to let me out.

"I can smell the ghost," she added. "It's a sort of geriatric smell. Sometimes he follows me around."

Roberts agreed. "Mary smelled him up on the second floor one night, and she said he'd followed her down. I could smell him, too."

"One night," Pete went on, "the staff here at the Tap had closed up and were sitting around the fireplace and they heard the door of the walk-in cooler open and shut in the basement. They went down to check and no one was there."

The two women agreed that paranormal activity seems to pick up in the autumn, though perhaps it's just more noticeable without the hustle and bustle of summer guests. Certainly the Belton Chalet offers a rare opportunity for ghost hunters who would like to spend a night or two skulking along creaking corridors, looking for ghosts.

My friend Sue had experienced what was probably paranormal interference with the plumbing in her room. Would I be as lucky, and manage to "bag" a ghost in this most haunted of inns? Well....

I had just turned off the light and settled into the comfortable bed when I saw a bright flash of white light near the ceiling by the door. A few years prior I had sat in the dark with a group of ghost hunters in a haunted theater. Once our eyes adjusted to the darkness, many of us had been able to watch orbs, those floating balls of light that are thought to be some form of paranormal energy, dart around. Could this be an orb?

I waited. The flash came again, from the same general location.

I poked Frank with an elbow. "Did you see that?" I hissed.

We waited tensely. There was another flash, and this time Frank saw it too.

"Turn on the light," he said calmly. I did. We both looked up at the corner where we had seen the flashes.

"It's a smoke detector!"

Even as we watched, the white light, tinged with red, flashed again.

My laughter was somewhat rueful. Here we were, in one of the most haunted buildings in Montana on the proverbial dark and stormy night, and I had only managed to bag a smoke detector!

Until, that is, we looked at our digital photos next day, and saw the large bright orb perched above our bedstead...

The Belton Chalet is surrounded by some of the grandest scenery in the world. Hikers, birdwatchers, and those who just want to get away from the stresses—but not the comforts—of modern life will enjoy a stay at the historic lodge. Ask for Room 37, if you dare. Who knows, perhaps the mysterious gentleman in the derby hat will pay you a visit.

TIPS FOR
GHOST HUNTERS

Would you like to try your luck as a ghost hunter?

It's not difficult to find a haunted site. Ghosts are most likely to be found wherever people have experienced strong emotions. As you might expect, battlefields are often haunted. Little Bighorn Battlefield National Monument near Hardin, Montana is one of the best known.

Spirits may linger near the sites of horrific murders, train wrecks, airplane crashes, and fatal automobile accidents. Hotels, bed-and-breakfast inns, theaters, lighthouses, saloons, schools, forts, museums, antiques shops, and even ships have been known to be haunted. In my experience, cemeteries are seldom haunted; ghosts are far more likely to be found in the places where they lived or died than where their bodies were buried.

Not every haunting is a result of tragic events. Some ghosts linger in their former homes or places of employment because they enjoyed their home or job so much that they can't bear to leave. Others may simply be confused, unaware that they have died, and so unable to move on. A residual haunting may not involve a spirit at all. That type of haunting is thought to be the result of emotional energy that has been absorbed by the fabric of buildings, particularly those built of stone or brick. A residual haunting can be distinguished from a haunting by an actual spirit because the same actions are repeated over and over and the "ghost" never interacts with observers.

If you can't find a haunted location to visit, contact your local chamber of commerce. Many towns offer ghost tours, particularly around Halloween. Or try your local newspaper office or historical society. They usually know of some reputedly haunted sites. Libraries may have information about haunted locations in their areas. And don't forget to ask security guards and maintenance workers about ghosts they may have encountered while working alone late at night in old buildings.

Many guides to haunted sites can be found on the internet. Try the American Ghost Society's website *www.prairieghosts.com* for information about ghost hunting, as well as a comprehensive catalog of books about ghosts.

Once you've chosen a place to visit, how should you prepare for your adventure? Here are some tips:

First, expect the unexpected. When my friends Pat Cody, Sue-Ellen Welfonder, and I held a night vigil at the Catfish Plantation in Texas, we had been told to expect dancing blue lights in the darkness. What we actually got were footsteps and the clattering of objects in the kitchen. Since we had not expected an audible haunting, we didn't have a tape recorder with us and so missed the chance to record and analyze the noises. Don't believe that ghosts are only active at night. Ghostly phenomena can occur at any time and may include footsteps, voices, raps on walls, temperature drops, moving shadows, pleasant fragrances or foul stenches, objects moving from one place to another, or, rarely, an actual apparition. One thing is certain, however—if anything happens, it will be when your attention has begun to wander!

Second, never go alone, particularly to isolated places. Ghosts won't cause you harm unless you panic and jump out a second-story window, but your fellow man can and may. Besides, anything you see or hear will be much more credible if you have a witness or two. Be sure someone knows where you are going and when you expect to return.

Third, if visiting haunted hotels, restaurants, and other public places, schedule your visit in advance. Be sure to note the name of the person with whom arrangements have been made. Be considerate: these places are businesses and their first priority is, of course, their customers. Thank them when you leave, not only as a matter of courtesy but because you may want to come back. It wouldn't hurt to patronize the business while you're there, either.

Fourth, dress properly for conditions. Few things spoil a "stakeout" more quickly than not being dressed for the weather. Sturdy, comfortable shoes are a must.

Fifth, practice with cameras, tape recorders, and other equipment until you are thoroughly familiar with them. An actual ghost hunt is not the best time to try to figure out how to run a new video camera or change batteries in your tape recorder.

Sixth, bring extra batteries for cameras and tape recorders—*lots* of batteries! Batteries can be quickly drained of power in haunted places. Cameras and tape recorders may jam or simply not work.

Seventh, never trespass on private property. It is always discourteous and in some states it is a felony.

Eighth, be careful about who you include on a ghost hunt. Practical jokes and rowdy behavior are inappropriate, distracting, and potentially dangerous in stressful situations. Novices should be paired with a more experienced investigator who won't panic at the first creaking floorboard or gust of cold wind. A paranormal researcher in England found that out the hard way when he agreed to take a man he'd never met on a vigil at a ruined castle. There was no electricity, so the ghost hunters settled down in separate areas to wait quietly in the darkness. The stranger grew more and more uneasy as the night progressed. The near-total darkness and isolation affected him so badly that he finally panicked and hurled himself through an open window ten feet above the ground. Luckily a shrub broke his fall, or the castle might have acquired a new ghost that night.

Paranormal phenomena can occur at any time of the day or night, so it is rarely necessary to hold a vigil in total darkness. If you must do so, protect yourself from potential injury by carrying a powerful flashlight. At Gettysburg recently, a female ghost hunter almost stepped into a deep hole while tramping through pitch-black woods. Fortunately her flashlight beam swept across the hole just in time to save her from injury.

Finally, be respectful. Ghosts are people. Pretend they're your Aunt Emma or Grandpa George and explain to the ghosts who you are and why you're there. Treat them as you'd like to be treated. You'll probably get better results if you do. Remember that people's personalities don't change just because they've died. Most are nice folks. A few are just plain nasty.

That brings up a question I've been asked occasionally: can a ghost harm you? I've heard firsthand reports of ghosts pushing people down the stairs and, in one case, slamming a car door on an investigator's leg, but I've never run into that situation myself. My personal belief is that you're probably in more danger from the living than from the dead. If you feel uneasy or threatened in any way, *leave immediately!*

Once you've arrived at your chosen site, how do you conduct an investigation? It depends on the circumstances. You may be lucky enough to have been able to arrange for a vigil in the haunted building. That won't happen very often, in my experience, because most owners are rightfully concerned about security and liability issues. If you're fortunate enough to get permission, you will likely want to bring all sorts of equipment. Technically oriented ghost hunters set up various types of cameras, thermal scanners, and electromagnetic field detectors, all hooked to computers. If you're an "intuitive" ghost hunter, a person who can sense the presence of spirits, you may just want to settle down in an area you feel is "active" and wait for something to happen. Ghostly phenomena don't occur on schedule, and never when you are expecting it. Many times nothing at all happens, and you end up with no more than a stiff neck. Professional ghost hunters have found that a certain amount of mental distraction seems to encourage phenomena, so they will often play cards during a vigil. Needless to say, don't drink or take drugs, and avoid smoking so cigarette smoke isn't mistaken for ghostly mists on photographs.

Even if you are denied permission to hold a vigil, some owners will give you a brief tour of the property or even allow you to roam around on your own. If so, see if they will allow you to use a tape recorder or camera on the premises. You may capture ghostly voices or shadowy figures.

Is it better to know everything about a haunting before visiting a site, or go in "cold?" The theory is that if you know what to expect, anything you may experience can be put down to wish fulfillment. We've tried it both ways, and don't believe the "wish fulfillment" theory is valid. If that were the case, our experiences would (or should) match what has been reported previously—and they rarely do.

Our usual procedure when beginning an investigation is to tour the site, either on our own or with one of the witnesses. We take photos on impulse, search for unexplained cold spots, and use tape recorders. If we get something unusual on film, we try to return to the site to take more photos for comparison. We always look for natural causes for apparent paranormal activity. Is that cold spot caused by a draft from an air conditioning vent? Do the stairs creak because the building is cooling after a hot day? Is an eerie scratching noise just a branch scraping across a window? Later, we interview those who have had experiences and are willing to speak about them. Do the witnesses seem credible? Do reports of the haunting go back many years? If so, the haunting is more likely to be genuine.

Is there a historical basis for the haunting? Always try to verify stories that are told. If someone was supposed to have hanged himself in a building, check with neighbors to see whether any of them recall such an occurrence. If not, a search through old newspaper indexes and microfilms may turn up information. Often nothing can be found.

We've often been asked whether a ghost can follow you home. It's unlikely, but not impossible. Most ghosts have an emotional attachment of some sort to the place they haunt and don't want to—or can't—leave. Occasionally, however, ghost hunters report that ghosts have followed them home. Sometimes the ghosts seem desperate for help, rapping on walls or moving objects to catch your attention. If you want to attempt what's called a rescue, try talking aloud to them. Explain that they have died; apparently many ghosts don't realize that they are no longer in their physical body. Mention the current date, and point out that many years have gone by since they died. Ask them to visualize a bright light and to move toward it, thinking of their loved ones who died previously. Usually that will be enough to help them cross over to the Other Side. If the ghost is reluctant to go, you may need to contact a medium who is experienced at rescue work.

As you gain experience you'll develop your own methods of investigating haunted places. Don't be afraid to experiment. Remember, there are no experts in this field. If you're an electronics wizard, you may want to set up computer networks to monitor ghostly activity. Perhaps you'll devote your vacation to exploring haunted battlefields or staying in haunted bed-and-breakfast inns. Or perhaps you prefer to just settle back in your armchair with a good ghost story and a cup of steaming tea, ready to experience a few pleasurable shivers.

However you choose to hunt your ghosts, enjoy!

ABOUT THE AUTHOR

I'm a reference librarian, one of those logical folk who enjoy ferreting out answers to difficult questions. An unanswered question is, to me, an irresistible challenge. That's why I find paranormal investigation so fascinating. Although I've studied paranormal phenomena for over 50 years, I still don't know how and why they occur. I have no doubt that they *do* occur, however, because when I was seven years old my family moved into a haunted house in Minneapolis. Over the years, everyone in my family had experiences we couldn't reasonably explain. To deny them was unthinkable; we'd have had to deny the evidence of our own senses.

My folks didn't know the three-story brick and stucco house was haunted when they bought it. The house had been built in 1920 for a Minneapolis businessman; from the outside it had an air of quiet distinction. It didn't take us long, however, to figure out that we shared our house with something or someone we couldn't see. At first it was just a sense of an invisible presence. For example, my folks had fixed up a playroom in the basement, but my sister and I never liked to play down there because we often felt that someone we couldn't see was standing in the doorway staring at us—and not pleasantly, either! We tried to ignore it, but eventually the feeling of dislike would grow so intense that we'd run upstairs to find our mother.

A few months after we moved in, we began to hear footsteps coming up the stairs from the basement. No one was ever there when we opened the door to look. My folks just shrugged it off. My dad was a very rational man, trained as a chemist, and he didn't believe us when my sister and I told him the house was haunted. Something happened one evening, though, that made even my father wonder. We were eating supper at the kitchen table, the door to the basement closed as usual. Suddenly the doorknob started to turn back and forth as if someone were standing on the other side of the door. My dad got quietly to his feet and yanked the door open. Nothing was there—nothing that we could see, that is. Dad was never able to explain that incident to his satisfaction, or ours.

Even as a youngster, I was insatiably curious. *How* could something without a physical body manage to flick on the dining room light? *Why* did we all hear footsteps coming up the basement stairs? *Who* rang the doorbell but left no tracks in fresh snow? My dad must have grown tired of the barrage of questions, but he never discouraged me from looking for answers.

When I was older, I rode my bike to the nearest branch library and practically devoured every book about ghosts. None seemed to have the answers I wanted, so I decided to experiment. I spent many hours trying to trap our ghost. Mom wasn't at all pleased about the flour I sprinkled on the basement floor (no, the ghost didn't leave footprints) and made me clean it up. When Dad tripped over the strand of yarn I had fastened across the basement steps and nearly fell headlong, my experiments came to an abrupt end.

We weren't the only ones who were aware of the ghost. My sister's dog Trixie often stood at the top of the basement stairs, looking down and growling. Although we could see nothing to alarm us, we trusted Trixie's instincts, and never went downstairs at such times.

As the years went by, the incidents became less frequent. Perhaps the ghost felt less need to make its presence known because we no longer used the playroom in the basement, or maybe it found teenagers less disturbing than children.

When I was about sixteen, however, I was reminded in no uncertain terms that our unseen watcher was still present. One Saturday morning I was home alone, ironing clothes in the basement. The radio was playing softly, and I certainly wasn't thinking about ghosts. After all, nothing had happened in quite a while. Then I heard the distinctive click of the light switch in the dining room and the sound of heavy footsteps crossing the room directly above me. As I looked up in surprise, I saw the exposed wooden beams actually sag as someone crossed the floor. I ran upstairs, expecting that one of my family had returned, but found no one at all. My folks drove up a half-hour later.

I never ironed alone in the basement again.

I lived in that house for 19 years before marrying and moving out. My folks and I often joked about "George," as we had named the ghost, but we never found an explanation for the haunting. After my father passed away, Mom sold the house and I seized the chance to examine the deed. I looked up obituaries for all the former owners and, as I had suspected, one of them had died in the house. I don't think she was the ghost though, because we all had the strong impression that the ghost was male.

I sometimes wonder if the current owners have heard the phantom footsteps. If they're not sensitive to the paranormal, they may have noticed nothing—and I'm not about to ask.

Perhaps my early experiences led me to a career as a researcher, historian, and ghost story collector. Along the way, I've spent many enjoyable days and nights roaming haunted castles, plantation houses, and abandoned prisons in search of ghosts. Often I've gone home with nothing to show for a night's vigil but a stiff neck and sore feet, but, looking back, I wouldn't have missed a moment of it.

May you too, enjoy many ghostly adventures!

Karen Stevens is the acquisitions librarian at the Parmly Billings Library in Billings, Montana. To contact her about a haunting, email kstevens@cs.com.